" To speed the word of God afresh in each age, in accordance with both the novelty of the age and the eternal antiquity of truth, this is what St. Paul means by 'interpreting the unknown tongue.' "—PÈRE GRATRY.

" He who wishes to understand the historical Jesus will have recourse to the witnesses who came under the first unmixed effects of the spirit of Jesus."—PROF. OTTO SEEBERG, University of Berlin.

THE POST-APOSTOLIC AGE

And Current Religious Problems.

BY

JUNIUS B. REMENSNYDER, D. D., LL. D.,

Author of "Heavenward," "Doom Eternal," "Six Days of Creation,"
"Lutheran Manual," "The Atonement and Modern Thought,"
"Mysticism," etc., etc.

WIPF & STOCK · Eugene, Oregon

Wipf and Stock Publishers
199 W 8th Ave, Suite 3
Eugene, OR 97401

The Post-Apostolic Age and Current Religious Problems
By Remensnyder, Junius B.
Softcover ISBN-13: 978-1-6667-6162-7
Hardcover ISBN-13: 978-1-6667-6163-4
eBook ISBN-13: 978-1-6667-6164-1
Publication date 10/10/2022
Previously published by Lutheran Publication Society, 1909

This edition is a scanned facsimile of the original edition published in 1909.

FOREWORD.

THE question of our time is whether the claim of Christianity to a special divine revelation is, or is not, authentic. No graver, more momentous issue was ever presented.

The peculiarity of the present is that a group of scholars in the Church is challenging the historical view of twenty centuries. Hence doubt as to the authority of the Scriptures and the certainty of the Christian faith is whispered from ear to ear.

And the multitude are saying: "Well, then, we will trouble ourselves little with either Bible or creed." As the practical result, there is a growing dissolution of the bonds of religion.

And the worst is, that, from this point of view, the multitude is right. If Christianity be true, it cannot undergo a *radical* change. Only the false can be torn up by the roots. Only the cancer must have the knife to the core.

Old truths must, indeed, recognize new truths and embrace them in a larger synthesis. For all truth, scientific as well as religious, is one. Nature and revelation, reason and faith dare not and cannot conflict. The old body of truth must wear new garments, fitted to the new issues made by progress and by modern thought and life. But while truth thus grows, develops, spreads, deepens, it is not by repudiation of, but by building upon, its past. What was true in Christianity as it fell from the lips of Christ and His inspired apostles, has been true ever since, is true to-day, and will be forever true.

From whatever source light can be thrown upon this vital question it should be welcome.

The aim of this volume is to show that the Christian faith, though varying in adaptation to the changing conditions of men and society, has ever preserved its essential identity. It has been, is, and will be, one. It has never cut from beneath it the foundations of antiquity and history. Its vital doctrines are generically the same to-day as they were interpreted by the generation in closest touch with its origin, and as they have been held these centuries. All the advances of modern progress and all the discoveries of science have not shaken one central pillar of this blessed edifice of the faith and hopes of man. Whatever else has passed away, or will pass away, Christianity, reared by the pierced hand of its Founder upon the Rock of Truth, endures. Only to such a religion, which can face unmoved the eternal years, can the soul entrust its immortal destiny.

NEW YORK, REFORMATION DAY, 1909.

CONTENTS.

CHAPTER I.
THE AGE SUCCEEDING CHRIST AND THE APOSTLES 11

CHAPTER II.
WHO WERE THE APOSTOLIC FATHERS? 16

CHAPTER III.
THEIR IDEA OF CHRISTIANITY—A REVELATION 24

CHAPTER IV.
THE CHRISTOLOGY OF THE APOSTOLIC FATHERS 26

CHAPTER V.
THE TRINITY 38

CHAPTER VI.
THE ATONEMENT 43

CHAPTER VII.
JUSTIFICATION BY FAITH 49

CHAPTER VIII.
THE NEW CHRISTIAN LIFE. 53

CHAPTER IX.
INSPIRATION OF THE SCRIPTURES 63

CHAPTER X.
BAPTISM. 72

CHAPTER XI.
THE LORD'S SUPPER. 81

CHAPTER XII.
THE HOLY CHRISTIAN CHURCH 88

CHAPTER XIII.
CHURCH GOVERNMENT AND POLITY 97

CHAPTER XIV.
THE CHRISTIAN MINISTRY. 102

CHAPTER XV.
AUTHORITY OF CHURCH MINISTRY 115

CHAPTER XVI.
CHRISTIANITY AND THE SUPERNATURAL—MIRACLES AND
  THE RESURRECTION 122

CHAPTER XVII.
THE APOSTOLIC FATHERS AND CURRENT VIEWS AS TO THE
  SUPERNATURAL 130

CHAPTER XVIII.
THE SUPERNATURAL FUNDAMENTAL TO RELIGION 142

CHAPTER XIX.
PROTESTANTISM VERSUS ROMANISM 154

CHAPTER XX.
THE PRIMITIVE CHURCH AND CHARITY. 163

CHAPTER XXI.
THE CHURCH AND SOCIAL REFORM. 173

CHAPTER XXII.
PRIMITIVE RITES OF PUBLIC WORSHIP. 189

CHAPTER XXIII.
JOY IN MARTYRDOM. THE CATACOMBS 201

CHAPTER XXIV.
EDUCATIONAL RELIGIOUS METHODS. THE EARLY CHURCH AND CHRISTIAN NURTURE 217

CHAPTER XXV.
THE END OF THE WORLD—OTHER-WORLDLINESS. 229

CHAPTER XXVI.
THE APOSTOLIC FATHERS AND THE FUTURE STATE 237

CHAPTER XXVII.
THE OLD FAITH AND THE "NEW THEOLOGY" 249

CONTENTS.

CHAPTER XXVIII.
THE OLD FAITH AND THE "NEW THEOLOGY"—CONTINUED. BACK TO CHRIST—CHRISTIAN DOGMA 269

CHAPTER XXIX.
THE CESSATION OF MIRACLES AND MODERN HEALING CLAIMS 284

CHAPTER XXX.
INFERIORITY OF THE PATRISTIC LITERATURE TO THE INSPIRED WRITINGS OF THE NEW TESTAMENT 296

CHAPTER XXXI.
GENERAL VIEW. LESSONS FOR THE PRESENT 303

CHAPTER XXXII.
GENERAL VIEW—CONTINUED. AUTHORITY OF THE POST-APOSTOLIC AGE 314

CHAPTER XXXIII.
GENERAL VIEW—CONCLUDED. ESSENTIAL IDENTITY OF PRIMITIVE AND MODERN CHRISTIANITY 322

The Post-Apostolic Age.

CHAPTER I.

THE AGE SUCCEEDING CHRIST AND THE APOSTLES.

A VISITOR of Ewald relates that the great theologian, taking in his hand a small volume of the Greek New Testament, said, "In this little book there is more wisdom and creative force than in all the libraries of the world."

Similarly writes Henry Van Dyke, D. D. "The literature of the world holds no other doctrine so limited in bulk, so limitless in meaning." *

And this because it depicted that unique fact of history—the origin of Christianity. That was the fullness of the times. The Christ then appeared. God was manifest in the flesh. Truth spoke with uncreated voice. At last light was cast on the troubled deep of human thought. Absolute authority solved the great problems of knowledge.

* "Gospel for an Age of Doubt," chap. v.

Sin, error and sorrow fled from the face of the only-begotten of the Father. The age-sealed walls between the visible and the invisible realm were parted. Supernatural powers shook and gleamed athwart the fixed frame of nature. The grave was opened. Death was abolished and life and immortality brought to light. It was the era in which was wrought out the drama of human redemption, in fulfillment of the eternal purpose of the Father.

No wonder, then, that all succeeding ages have looked back to it as the central era of history. And that to it all minds have turned for knowledge, for instruction, for help and for inspiration, with an intensity of interest such as no other era can incite. And that the literature, portraying that period, as contained in the gospels and epistles of the New Testament, is daily under every eye.

THE TIME NEAREST TO CHRIST.

But there is an epoch only second to this original one, in instruction and surpassing interest, and which is all too little known. This is the *post-apostolic age*. The time immediately succeeding the incarnation wonder. Christ has been crucified and ascended. The apostles have all departed. The authoritative preachers of the gospel are gone. The inspired representatives of Christianity are no more. The mighty pillars of the Church no longer uphold it.

Yet, departing, they bequeathed the great work to their successors. How incalculable was the responsibility thus committed to their hands! Their supreme task it was to interpret Christianity truly to their age, to defend it from the dire perils threatening it, and to transmit it in its purity to after generations.

To this seemingly superhuman task the Christian fathers of this period brought exceptional advantages. The Sun of Righteousness had set, but a great effulgence yet lingered on the horizon. The primitive Christian tradition abode in its first cast of absolute purity. They were men most, if not all of whom had known the apostles personally.

Take, for instance, the exquisite account which Irenaeus, in a letter to Florinus gives of the way in which he heard Polycarp discourse concerning Christ and the apostles : "When I was yet a child, I saw thee at Smyrna in Asia Minor, at Polycarp's house. I can more distinctly recollect things which happened then than others more recent ; for events which happened in infancy seem to grow with the mind, and to become part of ourselves; so that I can recall the very place where Polycarp used to sit and teach, his manner of speech, his mode of life, his appearance, the style of his address to the people, his frequent references to St. John and to others who had seen our Lord; how he used to repeat from memory their discourses, which he had heard from them concerning our Lord, His miracles and mode of teaching; and how, being instructed by those who were eye-witnesses of the word, there was in all that he said a strict agreement with the Scriptures."

THE PRIMITIVE FATHERS PROVIDENTIAL MEN.

In addition to these exceptional advantages, there can be no doubt that God, who calls the man for the hour, who gives the strength for the day, and who fits the hero for the occasion, specially endowed these leaders for their work. They were providential men. They had a special baptism of the Holy Ghost. The Lord "stood by them" in a remarkable manner. A *quasi*-inspiration strengthened them for the superhuman enterprise of successfully publishing the gospel to mankind and launching the ship of Christianity upon the surging sea of the world. And if, then, we make a constant and earnest study of the New Testament era, shall we neglect the study of this sub-apostolic age? Certainly none other is so closely in contact with, so rich in associations, traditions and instructions direct from the original source, and shines with so strongly a reflected light from the gospel sun as this. Truly does Guericke, in his "Manual of Christian Antiquity," say of it: "This period contains the basis of the whole development of the Church, to which whatever was of later origin attached itself as a mere accident of it." *

Fortunately, there is left behind a literature of this time. The writings of the representative apostolical fathers have been preserved sufficiently to give an accurate transcript of their thoughts. Let us, from a bird's-eye view of these precious written monuments, have placed before our minds a sketch of Christianity—the primitive Christian teaching and faith,—as conceived by the pious thinkers and leaders of the generation in immediate touch with the original founders.

* Chap. xii., p. 221.

CHAPTER II.

WHO WERE THE APOSTOLIC FATHERS?*

CLEMENS ROMANUS, called CLEMENT OF ROME, is one of the earliest writers of the post-apostolic age. According to the unbroken opinion of the primitive Church, and especially attested by Origen, Eusebius, Jerome, and others, he is the co-worker to whom Paul refers in Phil. iv. 3: "Whose name is in the Book of Life." This identity is confirmed by the judgment of modern scholarship. His epistle to the Church at Corinth may have been written as early as A. D. 75, certainly not later than 97. The "beloved disciple," St. John, was then still living, either at Patmos or in Ephesus.

Bishop Lightfoot thus fixes Clement's period. He says: "The date of the epistle was nearly simultaneous with the close of Diocletian's persecution, when the emperor's cousin, Flavius Clemens, the

---

* "The origin of the term 'Apostolic Fathers' should probably be traced to the idea of gathering together the literary remains of those who flourished in the age immediately succeeding the apostles, and who presumably, therefore, were their direct personal disciples."—"Apostolic Fathers," Lightfoot, ol. I., Introduction.

namesake of the writer, perished during or immediately after the year of his consulate, A. D. 95, and his wife Domitilla, Domitian's own niece, was driven into punishment on charges apparently connected with Christianity." *

Tertullian states that Clement was appointed by the Apostle Peter as overseer of the Church at Rome. He was a personality of almost apostolic force and influence, so that the early historian, Eusebius, states "that his epistles were publicly read in most of the Churches." † His epistles, therefore, were regarded on almost a level with the canonical writings. The Alexandrian Manuscript accordingly places this epistle in order the first after the inspired books.

Bishop S. Cleveland Coxe, in his edition of the "Ante-Nicene Fathers," writes: "The Epistle of Clement is the legacy of one who reflects the apostolic age in all the beauty and evangelical truth which were the first fruits of the Spirit's presence with the Church."

HERMAS.

This father's voluminous book, "The Pastor, or

* "Apostolic Fathers," Introduction, p. 3.
† "Ecclesiastical History," Vol. III., chap. xvi.

Shepherd," " was composed, most probably, in A. D. 97-100."* Hermas was generally believed in ancient times to be the person mentioned by the same name in Romans xvi. 14. The greatest Christian writers of the second and third centuries speak of his book as "divinely inspired." It, too, was read publicly in the churches. "The Pastor" of Hermas was more widely read by the primitive Christians than any other book except the New Testament. "It occupied a position analagous, in some respects, to that of Bunyan's 'Pilgrim's Progress' in modern times." It accordingly gives us an invaluable portraiture of the faith and devotional ideas prevalent among Christians of that period.

IGNATIUS.

The great bishop of Antioch at the time of the destruction of Jerusalem, A. D. 70. He suffered martyrdom at Rome, being thrown to wild beasts in the amphitheatre, December 20th, 107, a date ever after held sacred by the primitive Christians. Seven of his epistles to the early churches—Romans, Ephesians, Philadelphians, etc.,—are extant. " The Ignatian Epistles are an exceptionally good

* "Text-Book of History of Doctrines," Seeberg, Vol. I., p. 55.

training ground for the student of early Christian literature and history. They present in typical and instructive forms the most varied problems, textual, exegetical, doctrinal and historical. One who has thoroughly grasped these problems will be placed in possession of a master key which will open to him vast storehouses of knowledge."*

The ancient tradition, showing how close to that period he lived, had it that Ignatius was the little child whom Christ (Matthew xviii. 2), placed in the midst of the disciples as an example of innocence. His noble personality and saintly character were a mighty inspiration to the faithful in those sorely tried times.

POLYCARP.

This illustrious father, Tertullian states, was made bishop of Smyrna by St. John. According to the ancient tradition Ignatius and he were fellow-disciples of that apostle. His pupil, Irenæus, gives an exquisite picture of his boyish memory of this saintly man. As he recalls the times he sat at the feet of this companion of the apostles, we cannot but think what a precious legacy it would have

* "Apostolic Fathers," Lightfoot, Part II., Vol. I.

been had he written down some of these conversations, especially those describing the personal appearance of our Lord! But the tenor of them speaks in his epistle to the Philippians. When finally, at a great age, Polycarp was brought to the stake at Smyrna, to the entreaty of the proconsul that he should save himself by denying Christ, he answered: "Eighty and six years have I served Him, and how now can I blaspheme my King and Saviour?" and with this noble confession gave himself to the flames.

BARNABAS.

An epistle to the Church at large has come down to us from this apostolic father. All the external evidence points to him as being the Barnabas of the New Testament, St. Paul's companion and fellow-laborer. "No other name is ever hinted at in Christian antiquity as that of the writer."* The Vatican Manuscript of the Latin text has for its title, "Epistle of Barnabas, the Apostle." Origen even ranks it "among the sacred Scriptures. †

---

* Roberts and Donaldson, "Ante-Nicene Christian Library," Vol. I., p. 135.
† Com. on Rom., i. 24.

PAPIAS.

This father wrote five books, entitled "An Exposition of the Oracles of the Lord." His era was about A. D. 125. He was bishop of the Church in Hieropolis, and was martyred in Rome near A. D. 150. He had the friendship of Polycarp and with him had been a disciple of St. John, and had mingled with "others who had seen the Lord." His aim evidently was to gather and set down floating traditions of the Lord's sayings. Only fragments of his books, preserved by others, are extant.

THEIR METHODS OF GATHERING FACTS.

As showing the method used by the fathers of this period, who were writing for believers in far off times, we cite these words of Papias as to his care in gathering memorials of these sacred events: "I took pleasure but in those who rehearsed the commandments given by the Lord and proceeding from the truth itself. If, then, anyone who had attended on the apostles came, I asked minutely after their sayings—what Peter said, or what was said by John, or by Philip, or by Thomas, or by James, or by Matthew, or by any other of the Lord's disciples. For I thought that what was to be got from books was not so profitable to me as what came from the living voice."

"THE DIDACHE, OR TEACHING OF THE TWELVE APOSTLES."

The author of this treatise is unknown. As its name implies, it professes to give a summary of the teaching or message of the apostles, and incidentally reflects the Christian usages current at the time of its composition. Its date is fixed with great precision by the internal evidence. "No one," says Bishop Lightfoot, " could or would have forged it." * It bears every mark of originating in the immediate sub-apostolic age. Its vocabulary and style are those of the New Testament, as distinguished from classic or Patristic Greek. Its references to ecclesiastical customs, rites and practices, are pervaded with the atmosphere of the earliest Christian antiquity.

Quotations from the gospel of St. Matthew are frequent, but the four written and canonical gospels are unknown. Friday still bears the name —the " Preparation "—as in Scripture. The heresies of the second century—Ebionite and Gnostic—have not yet arisen.

* "Apostolic Fathers," Part II., Vol. I.

WHO WERE THE APOSTOLIC FATHERS? 23

It is earlier than Clement of Alexandria; earlier than the Shepherd of Hermas; and earlier than the Epistle of Barnabas, for all these quote from it; and it is older than Ignatius, for the ecclesiastical order at which he hints is not as yet existent. Its place in order of time, then, is immediately after Clement of Rome and Polycarp.

Its date, therefore, is most probably that assigned it by Lightfoot, from A. D. 70-90. It thus becomes one of the most authoritative of the Patristic writings, bearing the highest evidential value. "The Didache," wrote Professor Schaff, "fills a gap between the apostolic age and the Church of the second century, and sheds new light upon questions of doctrine, worship and discipline."

CHAPTER III.

THEIR IDEA OF CHRISTIANITY—A REVELATION.

It is evident that these writers, directly in touch with the original authors of Christianity, had a far greater opportunity than any other generation can ever have for learning the mind of Christ, for correctly imbibing the purport of the gospel, for truly divining the genius of Christianity. They virtually give us a sub-edition of the New Testament, a close-at-hand light thrown upon the great message. What, then, from their study of the sources, was their interpretation of Christianity? They considered it a REVELATION. They believed that a new religious era had appeared. A creative epoch in religion had arisen. After the silence of four centuries, God had spoken again to His people. A greater prophetic age than all others, that toward which the whole history of Israel led and which the great prophets of the past foretold, had come. A new religion is born. From the Old Testament comes the New; out of the decaying soil of Judaism springs Christianity. It comes not as an evolution of religious thought, or as the supreme flower of natural religion, but is emphatically a revelation. In it the heavens bend earthward and the eternal doors open. The Divine Spirit gives a new body of truth to men, undiscoverable by their reasoning powers. "The gospel came to us by historical tradition. It was not invented, it was preached. Christian inspiration never ceases to draw from it an indefinite progression of thought, but without ever breaking the historic unity which joins it to its origin." * This conviction of a positive revelation was at once the inspiration and power of the apostolic fathers.

* "Religions of Authority and of the Spirit," Sabatier, p. 242.

CHAPTER IV.

THE CHRISTOLOGY OF THE APOSTOLIC FATHERS.

THE chief constituent in this revelation is JESUS CHRIST. He is for them its beginning and end, its sum and center, its all in all. He is Himself the Revelation, and Christianity springs entirely from and is altogether molded by Him. Who, then, did they think Jesus Christ to be? *What is their Christology?* Their constant references to Him show an overpowering sense of His glory and majesty.

Thus, Clement of Rome, the friend of Paul, says: "Jesus Christ, the High Priest of all our offerings, the defender and helper of our infirmity. By Him the Lord has willed that we should taste of immortal knowledge, who being the brightness of His majesty, is by so much greater than the angels." *
"The grace of our Lord Jesus Christ be with you, through whom, be to Him glory, honor, power, majesty and eternal dominion from everlasting to everlasting. Amen." †

* First Epistle, chap. xxxvi.
† First Epistle, chap. lviii.

CHRISTOLOGY OF THE APOSTOLIC FATHERS. 27

The author of the Epistle to Diognetus writes: "The Father did not, as one might have imagined, send to men any servant, or ruler, or angel, but the very Creator and Fashioner of all things—by whom He made the heavens—by whom He enclosed the sea within its bounds—whose ordinances all the stars observe—from whom the sun has received the measure of his daily course."* Polycarp calls him "Son of God and High Priest—the only begotten, King forever, the Son of God, according to the Godhead and power, to whom be an everlasting throne." † He also states that from His seat "at the right hand of God He will return as the Judge of all the earth." Barnabas: "The glory of Jesus, for in Him and to Him are all things. Behold how David calleth Him Lord and the Son of God!" ‡ Barnabas, also, affirms His "pre-existence and divine creative activity." § Hermas: "The holy, pre-existent Spirit that created every creature. God made to dwell in the flesh." ‖ Ignatius: "And God, the Word, was truly born of

* Chap. vii.
† Epistle to Philippians, chap. xii.
‡ Chap. xii.
§ Epistle, chap. xii.
‖ Book III., "Similitude," v.

the Virgin, having clothed Himself with a body of like passions with our own." *

The apostolic fathers have also as vivid a conception of the humanity of Christ as of His divinity. He is truly God made flesh, taking upon Him all the infirmities and limitations and subjection to trial and need of human nature, by virtue of which self-emptying He is enabled to enter into closest living touch with men in every phase of human weakness and sorrow. Ignatius: "Christ is both fleshly and spiritual, born and unborn. God become incarnate, both from Mary and from God."†

Prayer is offered to Christ as God. Pliny, the younger, Roman governor of Judea, reports to the emperor that the Christians in their assemblies "were accustomed to sing a hymn of praise responsively to Christ as it were to God." Lucian, the Latin satirist, writes: "The Christians are still worshiping that great man who was crucified in Palestine." Justin Martyr writes: "We reasonably worship Jesus Christ, having learned that He is the Son of the true God Himself.‡

---

* Epistle to the Trallians, chap. x.
† Epistle to the Ephesians, chap. vii.
‡ "First Apology," chap. xiii.

The earliest liturgies, as those of St. James, St. Mark, St. Adaeus, St. Maris, and the Apostolical Constitutions, prove by their formulas of prayer that the worship of Christ was an essential feature of an ordered Church service.

THE DIVINE-HUMAN PERSON OF CHRIST.

These testimonies show that the integral feature of Christianity with our fathers was the Person of Christ. They regarded Him as divine. They did not look upon Him as the greatest of the prophets, or as the chief of the sons of men. But they ascribed to Him a true and essential divinity. They adored and prayed to Him as God. And this was the fact that first of all commanded their interest. It is the Lord's true and proper divinity that challenges their inquiry, demands their reverence, fixes their faith and settles their hope. Because of this unique characteristic they believe His word, bow to His authority, yield themselves to His service, and will die before they will deny Him. And in the assurance of this divinity of their Lord and Master will they confidently undertake the overthrow of infidelity, Paganism and Judaism, and the conversion of the whole world to His name.

Thus revering His person they are thrilled, also, with His MESSAGE. They regard Him as sent of God to publish the new covenant of grace. He reveals the love of the Father in a new degree. He brings to light life and immortality. He proclaims a universal brotherhood of man under the universal Fatherhood of God. He founds a religion not for Jews alone, but for Gentiles and the whole human race. He preaches a kingdom of God, in which religion is not one chiefly of ceremonies and of formal worship, but spiritual—a matter of the heart, a renewed soul, an inner life. And now that this gospel of good tidings is published, that this Door of Grace is opened, He calls upon all men to note the fullness of the times and to turn from the temporal to the eternal, from the earthly to the heavenly life.

But eagerly as they listened to the teaching of Him who spake as never man spake, not His message, nor His sinlessness, nor His supreme goodness, so made Him the object of their devotion as His self-revelation of the Divinity, that He was "God manifest in the flesh." It is charged by some critics that the Synoptics have not discovered this Deity, but that it is an invention of the philosophical tendency and mystical spirit of St. John. But whence, then, did the apostolic fathers get it? For the most of them—Clement, Barnabas and Polycarp, at least—wrote before John's Gospel had been written. Their proclamation of it proves beyond doubt that the divinity of Christ was the teaching of all the evangelists and was the common possession of the primitive believers. Not the faintest conception do we find here of Arianism. That, and not Christ's true divinity, was a later development. " 'The History of Doctrines,' if it is to understand the further development of Christianity, must keep this constantly before it as the starting point. It is one of the most certain facts of history that the thought and feeling of the apostolic age was based, not upon the man Jesus, but upon the Lord in heaven, who pervades and governs the universe, omnipotent and omniscient. It is simply absurd to attempt to explain in a psychological way, the immense impression made by the man Jesus, for no imagination could mistake the most powerful man for God." *

CUMULATIVE AUTHORITIES.

Canon Liddon, in a résumé of the teaching of

* "Text-Book of the History of Doctrines," Seeberg, Vol. I., p. 41.

the great Church leaders of the first three centuries, reaches the same conclusion. "A chain of representative writers, reaching from the sub-apostolic to the Nicene age, asserts in explicit language, the Church's belief that Jesus Christ is God. Thus Ignatius of Antioch dwells upon our Lord's divine nature as a possession of the Church and of individual Christians; he calls Jesus Christ "my God, our God." The sub-apostolic author of the "Letter to Diognetus" teaches that the Father hath sent to men the very Architect of all things on whom all depends. He has sent Him as being God. St. Polycarp appeals to Him as to the Everlasting Son of God; all things on earth and in heaven obey and worship Him. He is the Author of our justification, the Object of our hope. Justin Martyr maintains that the Word is the First-born of God, and so God. Tatian is aware that the Greeks deem the faith utter folly, but he nevertheless asserts that God has appeared in human form. St. Irenæus says: "If Christ is worshiped, if Christ forgives sin, if Christ is Mediator between God and men, this is because He is really a Divine Person. Clement speaks of the 'Living God who suffered and who is adored.' Origen maintains Christ's true divinity against the contemptuous criticisms of Celsus. Tertullian anticipates the Homoousion in terms. 'Christ,' he says, 'is called God by reason of His oneness of substance with God.' St. Cyprian argues that those who believe in Christ's power to make a temple of the human soul must needs believe in His divinity." And Liddon concludes: "This language of the preceding centuries does in effect and substance anticipate the Nicene decision." *

We may add here the affirmation of a modern divine of liberal tendencies. Dr. Henry Van Dyke, writing of this period, says: "If we are to have a Christianity which is real and historical, we must get into line with history. If we are to have behind us the power which comes from actual achievement in the world, we must understand the relation which it has always held to the Person of Christ. If we are to be in any sense the followers of the first Christians and to share the joy and peace and power of their religion, we must take the view they took of Jesus of Nazareth. Now the first Christians saw, and that the Church has always seen in Jesus Christ,

* Oxford Lectures on the Divinity of our Lord and Saviour Jesus Christ (Lecture VII., pp. 415-425).

a real incarnation of God, a true and personal unveiling of the Father, God in Christ reconciling the world unto Himself." * Hence His advent inaugurated a new historic era. The revelation of God to men inspired the race with new ideas, energies and hopes. Springtime blossomed such as man has never seen again, and its fragrance and life-giving power streamed through the universe as on a new creation morning.

CHRIST'S PERSONAL APPEARANCE.

A noteworthy feature of the sketch, which these writers give of Christianity, is that there is no attempt to draw other than a spiritual portrait of Christ. We have here nothing like the Gospel of the Infancy. Great as must have been the temptation to those who were setting forth so wonderful and unique a character, no mythical narratives, no extravagant stories, or trivialities mar their picture. We are not surprised that so few, if any, new sayings of the Lord are given. This fact simply shows that none but the directly inspired writers were held adequate to that, and that the gospels then written were considered so fixed and sacred that nothing could be added to or detracted from them.

* "The Gospel for an Age of Doubt," chap. vii.

But it seems strange and is the occasion for some disappointment, that, with all the facilities these writers had and with the eagerness with which they tell us they discoursed with those who had known the Lord, they do not give us some of those particulars which would be of priceless interest to all the Christian world. But never, through all these pages, is there a personal anecdote of the Saviour, or the least hint of how He looked, or any description of His physical person or appearance. Of all the legends and tales, which could not help by this period gathering like a mythical halo about the personal history of our Lord, not one is interwoven with these memorials. The same reticence on these points is observed as that maintained by the authors of the canonical Gospels.

This shows the poise, the sanity and the reverence of the apostolic fathers. And especially does it show that they were so vividly impressed by the transcendent glory of the divinity of Christ's person, as well as by the high redemptive purpose of His mission, that those features and marks of His humanity, which would be of such absorbing interest to our curious thought, were lost to view in their adoring gaze.

The Gospels are really not designed as personal biographies. But their intent was to set forth the Divine-Human personality, the authority as a revealer of truth, and the redemptive kingdom of Jesus Christ. They portray His word as an authority for the mind, as well as His conduct as an example for the life. They depict Him as living on and working with divine power as the Lord of Mankind. It is evident how totally irreconcilable their conceptions of Christ are with those of a representative of the extreme school of modern theological thought, viz., "Christ must be understood and explained after the manner in which all other things under the sun must be understood and explained, as the result of factors and forces that are also operative outside of Christianity. It has been impossible to understand Christ in this way in the past, because the deification of Jesus by the Church has made such an objective estimation of the founder of the Church impossible. It must now be the purpose of advanced theological thought to discard all that yet remains of the reactionary conservatism of former days in reference to Christ and His teachings." *

* Otto Pfleiderer, "Origin of Christianity."

The divinity of Christ, contrariwise, was with our fathers the chief and all-engrossing consideration. It glorified His humanity. It constituted the incarnation. It was the supreme basis for faith. In it lay the uniqueness of Christianity and the pledge of its world-conquering sway.

CHAPTER V.

THE TRINITY.

The consideration of the supernatural personality of Christ naturally forced to the front a question of momentous import. If Christ were truly God, and yet was the Son, what was His relation to the Father, and what to " the Holy Spirit who proceedeth from the Father "? This brought the apostolic fathers face to face with one of the most difficult problems of religion, and one of the profoundest depths of metaphysical thought. As a result, they elicited the doctrine of the Trinity.

In the Didache—Teaching of the Twelve Apostles—we find the Baptismal Formula in use co-ordinating the names of Father, Son and Holy Ghost as equally divine.*

At the close of the Epistle of Philo and Agathopus, describing the martyrdom of Polycarp, the language is used, "In Christ Jesus our Lord, by whom and with whom be glory and power to the Father, with the Holy Spirit forevermore. Amen."

* Chap. viii., sec. 3.

THE TRINITY. 39

Similarly the Epistle of the Church at Smyrna recites this last prayer of Polycarp: "O Lord God Almighty, the Father, I bless Thee, I glorify Thee along with the everlasting and heavenly Jesus Christ, Thy beloved Son, with whom, to Thee and the Holy Ghost be glory, both now and to all coming ages. Amen." Clement: "As God liveth, and Jesus Christ liveth, and the Holy Ghost liveth, who are the faith and hope of the elect,"—where the three sacred names are co-ordinated as in the Baptismal Formula. Justin Martyr: "Jesus Christ, the Son of the true God Himself, and holding Him in the second place, and the prophetic Spirit in the third." * In these citations divinity is expressly ascribed to the Father, the Son, and also to the Holy Spirit. Prayer is offered to each, and in speaking of divine acts and ceremonies a threefold source is ascribed to them. This is true in a much larger sense with the Son, but it is also the case with the Holy Spirit. "Faith in the God of Israel became faith in God the Father; added to this was faith in Jesus, the Christ and Son of God, and the witness of the gift of the Holy Spirit, *i. e.*, of the Spirit of God and Christ." †

* "First Apology," chap. xii.
† "History of Dogma in the First Generation of Christians," Harnack.

THE GREAT TRINAL MYSTERY.

The manner in which this unity of divine nature, and yet this trinity of person and acts, is to be reconciled has not escaped their attention. Yet they have not given it close study. The designation of God as Father, Son and Holy Ghost is preserved in connection with the Baptismal Formula, and is occasionally employed, but not made (especially as to the Holy Ghost) a subject of particular study.* They simply accept the fact and leave the mystery to faith.

More thought have they given to the unique Person of Christ. They recognize God as His Father, and on the human side the Virgin Birth. They, therefore, see in Him the Divine-Human, the God-Man. Yet, as to *how* the Son was generated by the Father; or in what manner the two natures blend in the Person, Jesus Christ; or how the properties of the divine and human natures can be united and yet distinct, or how they reciprocally influence one another, they have not reached a definite conclusion.

That the Son has always existed co-eternal with the Father; that He is the Logos, the Word, the

---
* "Apostolic Fathers," Seeberg, p. 78.

THE TRINITY. 41

Revealer of the Father; that God can be known only through the Son, and that He ever does the will of the Father, was their satisfactory and working conviction. Thus though they had taken up the Person of Christ, yet their Christology was not equal to that of Irenæus and Tertullian a generation later. There is no definite statement of the later formula of two natures in one person of Christ, nor of three co-eternal, co-equal persons united in one Godhead.

Nevertheless, that these formulæ were framed at a later period does not show that they originated then—for example, at the era of the Nicene Creed,—for we find the generic truths upon which they rest all here. Their roots and primary germs lie in the soil of this period. For we can distinctly see in the writings of the apostolic fathers the embryonic, if somewhat crude, efforts to give coherent statement to these great Christian realities, of which they had a vivid conception as facts, and yet whose mysteries it would require the deepest philosophy of the acutest minds of coming ages to formulate in as reasonable fashion as possible.

Their concern, however, with the doctrine of the Trinity is not metaphysical, but practical. They do not seek for it a philosophical definition, but find in it a fact most helpful to spiritual life. God the Father creating, ruling and governing in righteousness and love; God the Son, becoming incarnate and saving the world by offering Himself for its sin; and God the Holy Ghost, applying this redemption in the process of regeneration and the holy Christian life, make for them the indispensable need, the blessing and power of the Holy Trinity. Their use of the doctrine is eminently practical. "In all the forms of the Trinity, from the sharply defined tri-personal Trinity of Athanasius to the essentially tri-modal Trinity of Augustine, the great service it has rendered is not abstract nor philosophical. It is practical. It has protected the conviction that the real nature of God is revealed in Christ; it has justified the consciousness that the Spirit of Christ, animating the Christian life, is the Spirit of God; it has preserved the sense of real communion with God in Christ, which is the nerve of Christian worship."*

* Van Dyke, "Gospel for an Age of Doubt," chap. iii.

CHAPTER VI.

THE ATONEMENT.

A VIVID sense of sin pervades the consciousness of these early Christian writers. The holiness of God is brought into sharp contrast with the wickedness of men. The exceeding divine goodness and benignity make more repellent the sins and vices of the race. The human heart is seen to be alienated from God. Sin and immorality are regnant in society. The whole fabric of the Pagan world is morally corrupt. "Let us," writes Barnabas, "utterly flee from all the works of iniquity and let us hate the vices of the present time; let us not give loose reins to our souls that we should become like these. Let us utterly hate the works of wickedness." * On account of this universal sinfulness and degradation, the judgment of a righteous God has fallen upon men. A curse, infinite and eternal, impends over the guilty race.

But over against this doctrine of sin stands that of grace. Love in the Father's heart prompts to

* Epistle, chap. iv.

the world's rescue. Justice and wrath are to be circumvented by love and mercy. From these conditions issues the scheme of the *Atonement*. The incarnation is primarily conceived as a means of salvation. Jesus comes as the Revealer of the grace of God. But He not only publishes the new covenant of mercy, but He Himself is the means of the victory over sin. Sin is to be blotted out by forgiveness, but this remission is to be by His sacrificial blood. Here the apostolic fathers are at one with the New Testament epistles.

We cite: "Our Lord Jesus Christ, who for our sins suffered even unto death," * writes Polycarp; and again: "Let us then persevere in our hope, which is Jesus Christ, who bore our sins in His own body on the tree." † Clement: "Let us reverence the Lord Jesus Christ, whose blood was given for us." "He bore our iniquities. He carried our sins. He was an offering for our sins." ‡ Epistle to Diognetus: "He Himself took on Him the burden of our iniquities. He gave His own Son as a ransom for us, the Holy One for transgressors, the blameless

---

* Epistle, chap. i.
† Epistle, chap. viii.
‡ Epistle, chaps. xvi. and xxi.

One for the wicked, the incorruptible One for the corruptible." *

Barnabas: "For to this end the Lord suffered, that we might be sanctified through the remission of sins, which is effected by His blood of sprinkling." And again: "Christ also offered Himself as a sacrifice for our sins." † Ignatius: "Jesus Christ, who died for us in order that by believing in His death ye might escape from death." ‡ "Ignatius dwells frequently and with great emphasis on the 'blood' of Christ, 'the passion' of Christ, the 'cross' of Christ as an object of belief, a center of unity and a source of life." § "Clement speaks frequently of Jesus Christ as our High Priest, and with other additions which show the completeness of his conceptions on this point (sections 36, 61, 64). So the repeated mention of the blood of Christ (sections 7, 12, 21, 49, 55), with the references to ransom, deliverance, and the like, tells its own tale. Again, the constant repetition of the preposition διά, 'through Jesus Christ,' denotes the mediatorial channel."∥

* Epistle to Diognetus, chap. viii. † Epistle, chaps. v. and vii.
‡ "Epistle to Trallians," chap. ii.
§ "Apostolic Fathers," Lightfoot, Vol. I., p. 595.
∥ Ibid., Vol. I., p. 398.

THE ATONEMENT SUBSTITUTIONAL.

These strong, unqualified assertions are the utterances of a simple, deep and all-pervading certainty as to the fact that the mystery of the incarnation had for its chief intent the redemption of a lost world. Christ comes as Jesus—the Saviour from sin. He dies that He may save us from death, the penalty of sin. He bears the curse Himself, that we may be delivered from it. He sheds His blood, that our hearts sprinkled with it may be cleansed. He suffers on the cross the stroke of justice, that God may be just and yet forgive. He is made an "offering" and a "ransom" for us. He is the great "sacrifice" by which the guilty escape. He suffers in our stead. He identifies Himself with fallen humanity, that as its representative He may be its Deliverer.

"That Christ died on account of our sins was the apostolic tradition and the general belief. The death of Christ was universally regarded as the means by which we are transported into a new moral state of life, and this because Christ died the just for the unjust, in order that He might lead them into a new relation with God." *

---

* Seeberg, "Text-Book of the History of Doctrines," p. 47.

The broken law must be fulfilled, the guilt and penalty of sin must be borne by a spotlessly Righteous One and by an infinitely efficacious Redeemer.

The atonement is as fully the justification of God's unbending attitude toward sin as it is the redemption of the sinner. "It was the severity of Christ that made the agony of Christ, this love of God's holy law, even more than of His brother man. Do you realize how, first to last, He stood on God's side against men?"* And it was only when Christ had honored in full the holiness of God's claim upon the cross, that Paul could take the attitude to the law he did and speak of Christ as its end.

Certainly we have in these Patristic presentations no conception of the sufferings and death of Christ as limited to the influence of imitation or example. Nor is the more abstract problem particularly discussed as to how God could and did suffer. Nor do we have the substitutional nature of the sacrifice in the later Anselmian theory. But just as clearly and decisively as any theological statement could formulate them, we have the vital ideas of the doctrine of the atonement as a propitiation. As to this

* Forsyth, "Positive Preaching and Modern Mind," p. 147.

evangelical truth, as set forth in the inspired Scriptures, and as in course of time appearing in the great confessions of historic Christendom, they do not waver a moment. The incarnation for them has no religious value but as the background of the atonement. The cross is the key to the whole redemptive history. They believe with all their heart that, "First of all, Christ died for our sins according to the Scriptures." *

* 1 Cor. xv. 3.

CHAPTER VII.

JUSTIFICATION BY FAITH.

To participate in the redemption provided by the atonement, the fathers teach that Christ must be apprehended by faith. First of all, faith in Him as a Person. As the Son who revealed the loving heart and compassion of the Father. Faith reaching out to Him, laying hold upon Him and living in and through Him. Faith in Him as Lord, King and Shepherd.

But specifically faith in Christ as Saviour. As the One who, by His offering unto death on the cross, ransomed from sin, reconciled unto God, and restored the prodigal to sonship with the Father. It is this view of the Lord of Glory suffering for the sinner, that provides faith with its surety of forgiveness, as Polycarp writes, "The strong root of your faith is in our Lord Jesus Christ, who for our sins suffered even unto death." *

"It was just the death 'for our sins,' which confirmed the impression given by His Person and pro-

* Epistle to the Philippians, chap. i.

vided faith with a sure hold. He died as a sacrifice for us, and He now lives. His death had the nature of an expiatory sacrifice, for otherwise it would not have had strength to penetrate into that inner world in which sacrifices originated. But it was not a sacrifice in the same sense as others, or else it could not have put an end to them; it suppressed them by settling accounts with them; the validity of all material sacrifices was destroyed by Christ's death." * By this one great propitiatory offering we, making it our personal possession by faith, are justified. Thus writes Clement of Rome: "And we, too, being called by His will in Christ Jesus, are not justified by ourselves, nor by our own wisdom, or understanding, or godliness, or works, which we have wrought in holiness of heart; but by that faith through which Almighty God has justified." † This faith is not, however, merely the subjective grasp of the soul on the Person and work of Christ—the inclination of the heart in trust and love. But it is also faith objectively considered, not simply faith, but *the* faith. Not merely the faith that believes, but the faith that is

---

*"History of Dogma"—Laying the Foundation, Harnack.
† First Epistle, chap. **xxxii**.

JUSTIFICATION BY FAITH. 51

believed. Hence it is faith in the teachings of Christ, in the Word of Revelation, in the mysteries of the truth, in the common Christian confession. That justification, regeneration and salvation are effected by the merits of Christ through faith, instead of obtained by our own merits, are facts either assumed or expressly taught.

FAITH THE PRIMARY DUTY.

Not an echo is heard of the modern opinion, so potent with the world and often, more or less, affirmed by the clergy, that faith is a matter of indifference, that one needs but keep in view the regulation of his life, that if the aim be to live rightly it matters not what is believed. This view, to this primitive literature, is essentially un-Christian.*

It is true, however, that the doctrine of "justification through faith alone" is not laid down with the evangelical purity with which it was later ap-

* In Dr. Forsyth's recent Yale University Lectures, the following passage indicates the return to a more Scriptural conception : "It is not give and take ; it is all giving on God's part. He receives but what He gives and in His life we live. Our synergist pride is quelled as we realize that. Our self-satisfaction has its saving relief. We are no partners with God, fellow-workers as we may be. Our best faith, with all its works, is purely the gift of God, because it is aroused by His one gift, Jesus Christ."—"Positive Preaching and Modern Mind," p. 55.

prehended by Luther and wielded as the wand of might which revolutionized Christendom. Nor was it consistently maintained in its full application. Often it was conceived as that momentary act by which pardon was bestowed for all past sins. But thenceforward obedience was looked upon as meritorious, and the forgiveness of sins was not regarded in strict accord with Scripture teaching, as always and wholly dependent upon faith alone. Under the guidance of the Holy Spirit there is an evolution in the apprehension of divine truth. So the Augustinian conception of sin and grace is an advance upon that of this period, and still greater is that of Luther in this article of justification.

CHAPTER VIII.

THE NEW CHRISTIAN LIFE.

"THE beginning is faith, the end is love," wrote Ignatius.* That the believer was justified by faith, so far from relieving him from the necessity of good works, was to be their primary incentive. Faith was to be the fruitful root of the new Christian life of love. Thus Barnabas writes : " Having received the forgiveness of sins through faith in the Lord, we have become new creatures, formed again from the very beginning. Wherefore, in our habitation God truly dwells in us." † Here we have the relation of faith to life in the most intimate sense of gospel teaching. The Christian dynamic is a faith that finds expression in love.

THE LIFE OF THE ANCIENT WORLD.

The review of this period of the world shows three types of character or phases of life. One was that prevalent among the *Pagans*. This was

* Epistle to Ephesians, chap. xiv.
† Epistle, chap. xvi., "The Spiritual Temple of God."

that of skepticism in religion, profligacy of morals, selfishness, tyranny, avarice and cruelty. Those highest in the social scale revelled in the lowest and most degrading forms of vice. St. Paul gives a vivid picture of the shameless corruptions prevailing in his terrific indictment in the famous first chapter of Romans.

Farrar gives this graphic description of the Pagan morals, which is well worth transcribing: "The epoch which witnessed the early growth of Christianity was an epoch of which the horror and the degradation have rarely been equalled, and perhaps never exceeded, in the annals of mankind. The abundant proofs of this decadence of morals are stamped upon its coinage, cut on its gems, painted upon its chamber walls, sown broadcast over the pages of its poets, satirists and historians. I need but make a passing allusion to its enormous wealth; its unbounded self-indulgence; its coarse and tasteless luxury; its greedy avarice; its sense of insecurity and terror; its apathy, debauchery and cruelty; its hopeless fatalism; its unspeakable sadness and weariness; its strange extravagances alike of infidelity and superstition. Ostentation, caprice, gluttony, impurity, rioted in the heart of a society which knew of no other means by which to break the monotony of its weariness or to alleviate the anguish of its despair." *

> "On that hard Pagan world disgust
> And secret loathing fell;
> Deep weariness and sated lust
> Made human life a hell."

That this shameless and woeful state befell Pagan society at a time when mental culture was at its greatest strength and beauty, and when the immortal works of classic literature and art were produced, proves how impotent the natural reason is to save itself or to regenerate the world.

The second phase was that of *Judaism*. This, indeed, was in notable contrast to Pagan debauchery. It recognized the living God of the Old Testament. Its ideals were those of righteousness, justice and judgment to come. And it maintained an external piety and virtue. Nevertheless, it was largely a religion of legalism. Its horoscope was narrowed by a harsh bigotry. In common practice, it was self-satisfied with a religious observance of mere rites and ceremonies. Hence, even its most

* "The Early Days of Christianity," p. 4.

illustrious exponents were characterized by what has received the fitting epithet of Pharisaism. It utterly failed to frame men in the type of real piety and to invest them with the elusive charm of saintliness.

The third phase was that of the *Christian life*. This was totally new. It took its rise from the love of God in Christ. It was based upon the great fact "that God commendeth His love to us in this, that while we were yet sinners, Christ died for us." And so the believer's heart, warmed and suffused by his faith in this great truth, overflowed with love. He earnestly desired the good and welfare of his fellow, and was willing to sacrifice for his happiness. What a spectacle and reproof in that cold, hard, gloomy Pagan world this sweet Christian spirit of gentleness, meekness, patience and love! This was a life the Christian could not effect in himself, but it was the fruit of divine grace, wrought by the regenerating, recreative agency of the Holy Spirit. Christ is our life, in that He personally dwells in us, and works in us spiritual and eternal life. Here is felt the force of a great primitive experience—the Christ in us, who is our strength, who renews us in our hearts, and draws our hearts upward from this earth toward Himself.

THE IMITATION OF CHRIST.

The motive the early Christian kept before himself was the imitation of Christ. "How will you love Him who first so loved you? And if you truly love Christ, you will become an imitation of Him." * His love, His patience, His gentleness, and His self-forgetful sacrifice were ever in the thought of the disciple. The mind and temper of Jesus were the spirit of the new Christian life. And as its sources were faith and love, so was its outcome an intensely spiritual piety, the freedom of willing filial service rather than the constrained obedience of the slave.

Purity was the next distinctive trait of this life. The morality of the believer presented a shining contrast to Pagan impurity. The lives of the Christians were chaste, they were pure husbands and faithful wives. Their family circles were true homes, beautified and blessed by all the domestic virtues. The apostolic writers perpetually urge the grace of chastity, of which converts stood so eminently in need, amid the temptations of environing debauchery. The eleventh chapter of the ninth

* Epistle to Diognetus, chap. x.

Similitude of the "Shepherd," describing the association of Hermas and the pure virgins, is, perhaps, the most beautiful parable of chastity to be found in literature.

The cynical critic, Gibbon, is compelled to bear this testimony to the morals of the primitive Christians: "Their serious life, averse to the gay luxury of the age, inured them to chastity, temperance, economy, and all the sober domestic virtues. The contempt of the world exercised them in the habits of humility, meekness and patience. The strictest integrity and the fairest dealings removed the suspicions of the profane."*

Charity was one of the most marked of their qualities. "Let not widows and the poor be neglected. Be thou, after the Lord, their protector and friend," writes Ignatius.†

Clement writes: "He who takes upon himself the burden of his neighbor; he who is ready to benefit another who is deficient; he who becomes a distributor to the needy is an imitator of God."‡

This spirit of charity not alone breathes through

---

* "Decline and Fall of the Roman Empire," Vol. I., p. 546.
† Epistle to Polycarp, chap. iv.
‡ First Epistle, chap. xxxviii.

THE NEW CHRISTIAN LIFE. 59

all their writings, but it was illustrated in practical methods. Regular offerings were taken for the needy. Each church was held responsible for the care of its widows, orphans, sick and destitute. Instead of the Pagan selfishness and absolute indifference, the poor and the suffering were the objects of kindness, sympathy and care. Children and aged, instead of being exposed and left to perish in the most abject misery, after the Pagan fashion, were tenderly nursed and cheered by the ministries of love.

Hallam gives this testimony to this early custom of charity : " This eleemosynary spirit remarkably distinguishes Christianity from the moral systems of Greece and Rome, which were very deficient in general humanity and sympathy with suffering. Nor do we find in any single instance during ancient times those public institutions for the alleviation of human miseries which have long been scattered over every part of Europe.*

We find in this period, then, the seeds of that sweet spirit of charity which have taken root and flowered out into all those beneficent institutions of modern times, which afford such indescribable

* Hallam's " Middle Ages," p. 583.

relief and help to the children of sorrow, and which write the most glowing page in Christian civilization.

The new Christian life, taking its note from the cross, taught, also, the preciousness of sorrow. It had learned that by means of its discipline was evolved a depth of love, a height of heroism, a moral grandeur of soul and a fineness of spiritual beauty, which could never spring from the soft experiences of pleasure. "If Christianity lost the antique zest, the animal happiness, the naïvete of children who knew not the insufficiency of life, or that they shall love and lose and die, it gained a new potency in a sublime seriousness, that heroism that confronts destiny and that 'most musical, most melancholy' sadness which conveys a rarer beauty than the gladdest joy—the sadness of great souls, of Christ Himself, who wept often, but was rarely seen to smile. It discovers that if, indeed, our 'sweetest songs are those which tell of saddest thought,' it is better to suffer than to lose the power of suffering." * Thus, confronting that age-long problem of unvanquished evil and unrequited pain, in-

---

* "The Nature and Elements of Poetry," chap. v., Edmund Clarence Stedman.

stead of being driven to stoical hardness or despair, Christianity spanned this dark gulf of mystery with the goldern arch of God's ultimate purpose and thereby transformed it into a salutary discipline and added it to the blessings and triumphs of humanity.

CONTRAST OF THE CHRISTIAN LIFE.

Martineau thus eloquently points the contrast between the life originated by Christianity and the old world one: " The very center of gravity in human interests was changed. So great was the effect of this fresh power that you had only to step from the forum to the Church to find quite a new edition of human nature and a reversal of established sentiments and manners; in the young a reverence and simplicity ; in the slave a dignity and quietude ; in the woman a modest self-forgetfulness ; in the man a frank humanity, not ashamed to stoop to the smallest service or lift the voice in highest prayer ; all proclaiming that here an ideal of character and affection prevailed, quite different from the fevered and festering world on which the sunshine glittered without. I know not how anyone can appreciate these great changes without owning the presence of an intense divine agency." *

* " Seat of Authority in Religion," Book III., chap. i.

Such was the new spiritual life which Christ brought into the world and generated in the hearts of believers. This was the life that smote the Pagans with wonder. It was "the life hid with Christ in God." And it was this life—the outcome of faith—that was to conquer the world to the religion of Jesus of Nazareth.

CHAPTER IX.

INSPIRATION OF THE SCRIPTURES.

THE apostolic fathers, of course, received the Old Testament as the Word of God, but what was their view of the writings constituting the New Testament? There was no question with them as to the authority of Christ's words. These they regarded as truth, and hence infallible. The teaching of Christ—the gospel—they looked upon as that seed, which, quickened by the Holy Ghost, bore the fruit of the new spiritual life. Christ's words were truth, spirit and life. They were charged with regenerative force. They were the chief means of grace. "At the close of the apostolic era," says Ferris, in "The Formation of the New Testament," "authority was recognized in any saying or tradition which embodied the spirit of the Lord."

But how was it to be determined what were the words of the Lord? He left no written record. Oral testimony is ever unreliable. The most careful and reverent memory is liable to err. The primitive fathers as we have seen, resorted to every means to learn most accurately of Christ and His teachings from eye-witnesses and auditors. But in a matter of such primary moment as having the Divine Word absolutely correct and pure, oral methods could not be perfectly satisfactory or conclusive.

ORIGIN OF THE GOSPELS.

At first, however, the words of our Lord were but preserved by tradition. His sayings were treasured in the memories of the disciples with the greatest reverence. They, doubtless, compared and rehearsed these under the guidance of that Holy Spirit of whom Jesus had promised " He shall guide you into all truth," and " He shall bring all things to your remembrance whatsoever I have said unto you." * Thus, by degrees, a tradition, common in main outline, was evolved. Then, the evangelists sat down to write out their several memorials, differentiated by their individualities. Thus originated our Gospels. Paul, then, "not in the words which man's wisdom teacheth, but in the words which the Holy Ghost teacheth," † added his Epistles, as did the other writers.

The following dates may be accepted as approxi-

---

* John xiv. 26. † 1 Cor. i. 13.

mately correct as to the times when the different books of the New Testament were written: Matthew, between the years 55 and 65; Mark, between the years 63 and 70; Luke, between the years 55 and 58; John, toward the latter part of the century; Acts of the Apostles, about the year 63; Romans, 1 and 2 Cor. and Gal., about the year 58; Eph., Phil., Col., Philemon, about the year 62; 1 and 2 Tim. and Titus and Heb., about the year 67; Peter (Epistles), about the year 58 to 63; James (Epistle), about the year 48; John (Epistles), about the year 85; 1 and 2 Thes., about the year 52, or within twenty years after the resurrection of Christ; Revelation, about the year 95. And, as the Apostle John lived until the close of the first century, the early Christian churches had ample opportunity to inquire of him concerning the genuineness and authenticity of all the books of the New Testament.

Now, the question of vital moment for us is, what attitude did these great leaders of the generation next to Christ take to these writings? There was, as yet, no established canon. Neither the Church nor any authoritative tribunal had passed any verdict upon them. Our answer is found with absolute decisiveness in their literature. They quote from the Gospels, especially the earliest of St. Matthew [that of St. John, which was written a generation later, had not appeared when some of them wrote] and the Epistles of Paul, *as Holy Scripture*, regarding them the word of God just as they do the Old Testament.

Barnabas is the first to preface these citations with the phrase, "As it is written." Ignatius also writes: "When I heard some saying, 'If I do not find it in the originals, in the gospel, I do not believe,' and when I said to them, 'It is written,' they answered me, 'That settles it.'" * So Clement, making a citation from Paul's First Epistle to the Corinthians, applies to it the term, "Inspiration." † And Papias states that Mark wrote his life of Christ by dictation from St. Peter, and concludes: "Wherefore Mark made no mistake in thus writing, for he took especial care not to omit anything of the Lord's sayings he had heard, and not to put anything fictitious into the statement."

We append a few instances of citations:

Barnabas: "As it is written, 'Many are called, but few are chosen'" (Matt. xx. 16).† Ignatius:

---

* Epistle to Philadelphians, chap. viii.
† Epistle, chap. iv.

INSPIRATION OF THE SCRIPTURES. 67

"Handle me and see, for a spirit hath not flesh and blood, as ye see me have" (Luke xxiv. 39).* Papias: "In my Father's house are many mansions" (John xiv. 2). And a notable one from Polycarp: "I trust that ye are well versed in the sacred Scriptures. It is declared, then, in these Scriptures, 'Be ye angry and sin not' (Ps. iv. 5); and, 'Let not the sun go down upon your wrath'" (Ephes. iv. 26).† Here not only is the phrase "sacred Scripture" applied to Paul's epistles, but they are placed on an exact parallel with the Old Testament.

AUTHORITY FOR NEW TESTAMENT WRITINGS.

These citations from the Gospels and Epistles run all through the fathers. In fact, the warp and woof of their writings are made up of them. They are so interwoven as to form their very texture. And in making these citations it is evident by their manner that not the faintest shadow of doubt has ever entered their minds as to the authenticity of the writings making up the gospel deposit, or as to their authority as inspired by the Holy Ghost.

* Epistle to Smyrneans, chap. iv.
† Epistle, chap. xii.

Treating of this period, writes Seeberg: "That such was the esteem in which the writings of the apostles were held is confirmed by the facts that the documents which we have just examined abound throughout in references to nearly all the New Testament books, and that the latter, as well as the Gospels themselves, were read in the assemblies for worship." *

And writes Bishop Lightfoot: "The reception of the Gospels by the early Church was immediate and universal. They never were placed for a moment in the same category with the spurious documents which soon sprang up after them. In external history, as in internal character, they differ entirely from the apocryphal gospels, which, though in some cases bearing the name and pretending to contain the teachings of an apostle, were *never recognized as apostolic.* Upon the authenticity, *i. e.*, the apostolicity of our Gospels, rests their claim to inspiration." †

How, we may ask, was it that so unqualified an acceptance was given these writings, when, as yet, the canon of the New Testament was not definitely

* "Text-Book of the History of Doctrines," p. 82.
† "New Testament Prologomena," chap. i., sec. 6.

formed or closed? The answer is that if there was no formal, there was yet a virtual canon. Those writings which were held to be inspired were fixed by the universal consent of the Christians of the time. Later, when doubts and cavils began to arise, it became necessary for an authoritative ecclesiastical tribunal, expressing the concurrent opinion of the Church, to fix the limits of the canon—to decide what it should include and what exclude. And so also, when disputes began to originate respecting the meaning of Scripture, there, says Harnack, rose "the need of a fixed outward standard, in order to be able to disprove false doctrines, and to be able to maintain the true conception as apostolic doctrine." * From this need originated by degrees the Apostles', and then the other great historic creeds. They were all, as Forest shows in his "Christ of History and Experience," defensive, forced upon the Church by the necessity of definitely interpreting the Scripture, to save it from being wrested to the support of soul-destroying heresies. Hence, they were not, as is often charged, metaphysical formulas, but expressions of practical need.

* "History of Dogma," p. 86.

MEANING FOR OUR TIME.

This reverence of these apostolic writers for the Scriptures of the New Testament is of vital import for our time. When so many are in grave doubt, unsettled as to how much or how little authority to attribute to what has always been received as the Word of God, all shaken as to whether the sands under their feet are shifty or no, how strengthening to look back to this ancient period, when such opportunities as our modern age can never have existed for solving the question, and find the absolute certainty that in the Scriptures we have a veritable divine revelation on which we can repose our faith and hope with unbroken assurance.

Nor did that modern theory of a continuous revelation ever occur to our authors. They believed that the inspiration which indicted the Holy Scriptures was unique. Sabatier gives this expression to this claim of many current writers: "Inspiration is in the essence of faith. All Christians have their part in it. This state of inspiration as a common and permanent privilege, a transference from the exterior domain [the canonical Scriptures] to the conscience, is the vital point of the antithesis between the religion of the letter

INSPIRATION OF THE SCRIPTURES. 71

and the religion of the Spirit." * It is evident that this was not the point of view of the apostolic fathers. And, as to it, the question naturally arises, Why, with this immediate inspiration of the Spirit on the human mind and conscience, aided by the vivid light of modern progress, discovery, science, philosophy, archæology and ethics, not an additional sentence or line—to say nothing of a book—has been written to take place and rank with this revelation, originated nearly twenty centuries ago? This is its sufficient refutation. Facts are stronger than theories.

* " Religions of Authority and of the Spirit," p. 308.

CHAPTER X.

BAPTISM.

The sacraments of Baptism and the Lord's Supper occupy a prominent place in the Patristic literature. Baptism was regarded as essential to Christian discipleship, both on account of its institution by Christ and as the door of admission into the kingdom of God.

But it was esteemed not merely for these external reasons, but also on account of its objective efficacy. It was not only a sign, but a seal of the blessings of the covenant. It was at once a symbol and an instrument. The cleansing which the washing with water taught in figure, it also wrought in spiritual purification.

Their views are in perfect accord with the teaching of St. Paul that the ordinance is " the washing of regeneration and renewing of the Holy Ghost " (Tit. iii. 5). Thus Barnabas argues that the remission of sins procured by the cross is applied through the water of baptism, and says that before baptism " we are full of sins and defilement, but afterward have faith in Christ and the fear of God, and fruit in our hearts, and shall live forever." * And Ignatius writes: "Let your baptism be your armor, panopling you with faith as your helmet, with love as your spear, and with patience as a complete defence." †

Clement says: "The Christian should preserve his baptism without stain. It has publicly cleansed him from his sins." ‡ And he calls it a "seal" of this forgiveness. Barnabas says that he "who has thus received through baptism the forgiveness of sins and the renewing indwelling of God will fulfill the new law of Christ." §

From such and similar passages it is evident that baptism was, in their opinion, much more than an ecclesiastical rite, imprinting a formal label of Christianity, and that it had a direct, objective efficacy for the recipient. It offered remission of sin, and caused the subject to be born again unto spiritual and eternal life.

Writes the Reformed theologian, Hagenbach, in his "History of Doctrines": "Like the apostles, the first teachers of the Church regarded baptism

* Epistle, chap. xi.   † Epistle to Polycarp, chap. vi.
‡ Homily, chap. vi., sec. 9.   § Epistle, chaps. vi., xi.

not as a mere ritual act, but as having its objective results. It was to them not merely a significant symbol, representing to the senses the internal consecration and renewal of the soul, but an efficacious medium for really conveying to believers the blessings of the gospel, and especially the benefits of the sacrificial death of Christ."*

And Guericke, the Lutheran historian, says: "The Lutheran Church has followed the ancient tradition in retaining the formula for the renunciation of the devil, as a sign and a testimonial that those who through the laver of regeneration and renewing of the Holy Ghost enter the kingdom of God are thereby at the same time emancipated from the power of Satan." †

It was by reason of this assurance of spiritual cleansing and re-creation in the divine life, as connected with baptism, that these fathers placed so high an import upon it, that it was a subject of such rich suggestion to them, and that it clothed them with such a panoply of defensive armor in their Christian warfare.

THE BAPTISMAL CONFESSION.

In the administration of the rite, a public con-

* Vol. I., p. 198.   † "Christian Antiquities," p. 226.

fession of faith was demanded. This, in the first instance, was simply that of the trinal confession instituted by our Lord (Matt. xxviii. 20).

But to make the truth more emphatic, that faith was insisted on as a fundamental act for the reception of grace, this confession was developed by degrees into the Apostles' Creed. "These writings," says Seeberg, "indicate the existence of a baptismal confession in the early apostolic age."[*] Irenæus and Tertullian declare that this "rule of truth" has been "identical and everywhere employed in the Church since the time of the apostles." It was at first unwritten and transmitted by oral recitation as a means of defence against persecution and those who would betray the mysteries of the Church. This accounts for its written form not appearing until a later period. But "the contents of the Apostles' Creed, used as the primitive baptismal confession are incontestably of apostolical origin."[†]

IMMERSION AND AFFUSION.

The *mode* of baptism in common usage seems to have been that of a trine immersion. But two

[*] "Text-Book of History of Doctrines," p. 85.
[†] Guericke's "Christian Antiquities," p. 228.

references to it have been discovered by the writer. One by Barnabas, viz., "This meaneth that we, indeed, descend into the water, . . . but come up,"* where the reference is to baptism and that by immersion. The other is in the "Didache," or Teaching of the Twelve Apostles. It runs: "Baptize into the name of the Father, and of the Son, and of the Holy Spirit, in living (probably, running) water. But if thou have not living water, baptize into other water. But if thou have not either, pour out water thrice upon the head." † Here either immersion or pouring is recognized as an authorized mode. From this it would appear that one mode was not so fixed by apostolic practice but that it could be varied. And as the dispersion of Christianity throughout the various climates of the globe made pouring or sprinkling more feasible, that method came into general practice concerning baptism.

"Cyprian argues the whole case out with respect to the baptism of the sick by affusion. No contrary voice is ever raised; but in various ways a full body of testimony is borne to the unhesitating acceptance throughout the early Church of baptism by affusion as equally valid with that by immer-

---

* Epistle, chap. xi. † Chap. vii.

sion. And, despite the consentient testimony of the literature of the period to immersion as normal baptism, the entire testimony of the monuments is to the opposite effect. This makes it clear that from the second century down baptism as actually administered was not an immersion but an affusion, although ordinarily apparently affusion upon a recipient standing in shallow water." * Throughout, then, the whole Patristic period the validity of baptism by pouring or sprinkling was not questioned.

ADULT OR INFANT BAPTISM?

There is no reference to the question whether baptism should be administered to *infants*. Origen, a century later, writes: "The Church has received the tradition from the apostles that infants should be baptized." † Had adult baptism alone been originally instituted, we are at a loss to conceive how, with the obedient reverence with which rites instituted by Christ were venerated, so radical a change could have been introduced. Hence, although we find no instances recorded of it in this

---

* The New Schaff-Herzog " Encyclopedia of Religious Knowledge," Vol. I., p. 449.
† Epistle to the Romans, chap. v.

primitive literature, there must, as Origen declares, have been apostolical precedent for it. "Without some apostolical tradition," writes Guericke, "it is wholly inconceivable how its claim to an apostolical origin could ever have gained such unhesitating assent as it received from Origen. But, besides, we find the practice of infant baptism generally adopted even in the second century." * The Apostolical Constitutions thus speak of it as an apostolical injunction.

The conception of infant baptism seems to be of the essence of baptism. It was established as a means of introduction into the covenant and Church of God. But as there was a Jewish rite for the admission of children in the Old Testament dispensation, how natural that there should be a Christian rite for their reception in the new and larger covenant of grace! Baptism, again, was established for cleansing from sin. And shall the adult alone be cleansed and the individually innocent child be left with the taint of original sin, inevitably to develop into actual? And if it be said that faith is essential to receptivity for grace, does not Christ speak of infant faith;—"Of these little ones which

* "Christian Antiquities," sec. 31.

believe in me " (Matt. xviii. 6)? For if there be a sub-conscious sin, may there not be a sub-conscious faith ? And if the infant without its fault is stained with sin's evil dye, is it not but in accordance with divine justice and goodness that its sinful state should be cleansed without its personal act?

Moreover, baptism is the sacrament of the new birth, which Christ declares must take place before one can enter into the kingdom of heaven. And shall then the infant be denied that ordinance which is necessary to implant within it the germs whence shall develop the new life? Hence we conclude with Irenæus: " Christ came to redeem all by Himself: all who through Him are regenerated to God ; infants, little children, young and old." * And with the great church historian Neander: "In the child born in a Christian family, the idea of Christianity was that the new birth was not to constitute a new crisis, beginning at some definable moment, but it was to begin imperceptibly and so proceed through the whole life. Hence baptism, the visible sign of regeneration, was to be given at the very outset ; the child was to be consecrated to the Redeemer from the beginning of its life. From this idea,

---

* II., chap. xxii., sec. 4.

founded on what is inmost in Christianity, becoming predominant in the feelings of Christians, resulted the practice of infant baptism." *

But however true this line of reasoning, the question—one of so great practical moment—is not settled, one way or the other, in the works of the Patristic fathers. Apparently there is neither direct nor indirect reference to it.

* "History of the Christian Religion and Church," Vol. I., p. 312.

CHAPTER XI.

THE LORD'S SUPPER.

THE writings of the apostolic fathers show the profound impression which this ordinance had made upon them, the reverent regard in which they held it and the weighty blessings which they attached to its observance. We find no trace of such a conception of it as that of Professor McGiffert, viz., that it was merely designed as a farewell meal of fellowship and love. But their writings prove that it existed among them as a permanent rite, instituted by the Lord Jesus for His Church to observe to the end of time.

The references to it show also that it was held to be for more than a memorial of the death of Christ. The words of institution were so direct, simple and emphatic, that, with St. Paul, the fathers rejected a merely figurative interpretation of them. The fourfold iteration of the identical formula of institution of which Dean Stanley wrote: "These famous words thus form the most incontestable and the most authentic speech of the Founder of our religion," * convinced them of an objective reality in the ordinance. They look upon it first, indeed, as a confession,—a testimony to the sacrificial death of Christ—a public witnessing of their faith in Him who was a propitiation for the sins of the whole world. The celebration of the Lord's Supper is " the Church's confession to the world—the conquering power of the death of Christ."

THE REAL PRESENCE.

But further, they see in it a sacrament, a holy mystery. They believe that, more than a memorial and a confession, it has a supernatural aspect, it conceals a divine grace. This mystery presents no objection to their minds, more than does the Incarnation, or the Trinity. In fact, it is the characteristic of Christianity that the natural and the supernatural, the material and the spiritual, the earthly and the heavenly, should thus be held in inexplicable union. And the mystery in the Lord's Supper was that, with the bread and wine, were somehow united the body and blood of Christ, so that in receiving one the other was likewise received. It was, as St. Paul had termed it, a

* "Early Christian Institutions," p. 95.

"communion" [literally 'participation'] of the body and blood of Christ."* Thus Ignatius: "The eucharist is the flesh of our Saviour Jesus Christ, which suffered for our sins."† So the Didache: "Thou dost here freely give spiritual food and drink and life eternal through Thy servant."‡ This view concurs with that of the later father, Justin: "We have been taught that the food blessed by the word of prayer is also the body and blood of the same Jesus, who was made flesh."§ And of Tertullian: "The eucharist consists of two things, the earthly and the heavenly." ||

With regard to its effect, the forgiveness of sins, therein conveyed to the believing recipient, bestowed also life, spiritual and eternal. Thus Ignatius: "Breaking one and the same bread, which is the medicine of immortality and the antidote that we might not die, but live in Jesus Christ forever."¶ Harnack recognizes this aspect of their views in these words: "The Lord's Supper was viewed as 'medicine of immortality,' as a mysterious communication of knowledge and life."** So the

* 1 Cor. x. 16. † Epistle to Smyrneans, chap. vii.
‡ Chap. ix. § Chap i. 66.
|| IV., xvii. 5. ¶ Epistle to Ephesians, chap. xx.
** "Text-Book of History of Doctrines," p. 56.

historian, Neander: "The most common representation of the Lord's Supper was as the means of a spiritual, corporeal communion with Christ."* Hagenbach: "The Christian Church attached, from the earliest period, a high and mysterious import to the bread and wine used in the Lord's Supper." † The modern view, entertained in many quarters, of a merely memorial or figurative character, is excluded by the whole tenor of the Patristic teaching. The post-apostolic age knew nothing of it.

THE FATHERS REJECT TRANSUBSTANTIATION.

Was this doctrine the Roman Catholic one of transubstantiation? Evidently it was not. Transubstantiation is an attempt to explain the mystery. A miracle is wrought—the bread and wine become the body and blood of Christ as it had hung upon the cross, and while the miracle is present the mystery is solved. The idea in transubstantiation also is that by this change the bloody sacrifice may be repeated and offered up to God. Hence, also, the elevation of the host and adoration. But the Lord's Supper with the fathers is *not a sacrifice*, a something offered by man to God. It is contrariwise,

* "Church History," Vol. I., p. 647.
† "History of Doctrines," Vol. I., p. 204.

THE LORD'S SUPPER. 85

a *sacrament*, a something given by God to man— the communication of a divine grace. That the Lord's Supper was a sacrifice to be re-offered at the altar was originated at a later period by Cyprian: "The priest acts in the stead of Christ, imitating that which Christ did and offering a full and true sacrifice in the Church to God the Father." *

No suggestion of such Romish teaching appears in these fathers. Rather does their doctrine seem to be that of the reformers, especially that of Luther, viz., the real presence. This is not to be confounded with consubstantiation,—a mingling of the earthly and heavenly elements,—which Luther opposed quite as much as he did transubstantiation. The real presence distinguishes from the Romish doctrine of a change of the bread and wine, and also from a figurative or non-real presence. Gieseler, the eminent Church historian, concludes that this was the primitive view. He says: "The idea which lies at the basis of most of the statements about the Lord's Supper is, that as the Logos was once united with the flesh, so in the Supper it is now united with the bread and wine." † This believes and holds to the verity of Christ's words of

* Ep. lxiii. 14. † "History," p. 408.

institution, and while recognizing the testimony of the senses that the bread and wine remain unchanged, is assured of a holy mystery, a sacramental union by which, through the elements as an unconfused medium, the body and blood of our Lord are received to the remission of sins, to the strengthening in grace and to the communication of immortal life.

No one was allowed to partake of the Lord's Supper unless he had been baptized. Thus the rule is prescribed in the Didache: "Let no one eat or drink of the eucharist but they who have been baptized into the name of the Lord." * Confession was demanded before participation. This shows the vivid sense of sin and the intimate connection of the sacrament with the forgiveness of sins. Fasting was also usual in connecting with the preparatory discipline of penitence. The ancient liturgies abound with warnings against unworthy partaking and with exhortations that the communion should be taken fasting. † The sacrament was observed frequently [every Lord's Day in the earliest period], and was universally regarded as the most sacred

* Chap. x.
† "Constitutions of the Apostles," chap. viii. 12.

Christian ordinance, the highest and holiest feature of public worship and a most precious means of grace. This spiritual power came to it alone through the words of institution. It was, therefore, the specialization of the word, and the individual application of the grace offered by it. The word remains the chief means of grace.

CHAPTER XII.

THE HOLY CHRISTIAN CHURCH.

CHRIST came to regenerate the individual man. But He remembered that man did not live alone. He was a social being, the member of a community. And his highest well-being could only be attained when united with his fellow-man, one mutually influencing and perfecting the other. Thus the spiritual leaven was to change all men and Christianity to be for the whole world.

But to affect this there must be a Christian society, an organization. Hence from the very first we read that Christ came preaching "the gospel of the kingdom." Its citizens were to be regenerate souls, its spirit righteousness and love, and its Head the Lord Jesus Christ. This kingdom, society and brotherhood, He called the Church. But this Church,—in its inner constitution, spiritual and invisible,—to be an efficient working force in the world must realize itself in a visible form. And so He constituted the Church as visible, founded upon the word and sacraments. "Upon this Rock [the

THE HOLY CHRISTIAN CHURCH. 89

truth of His divine Sonship] I will build my Church, and the gates of hell shall not prevail against it." * Its purpose was that, by preaching the word and administering the sacraments, through them, as means of grace, the Holy Ghost should build up Christians in the spiritual life, who, working together, should spread abroad the gospel of the kingdom. It was thus to be a holy and a universal Church, a spiritual empire transforming all the peoples of the earth and bearing everywhere the sceptre of righteousness and peace. Its primary aim was salvation. " He that believeth and is baptized shall be saved," † was Christ's declaration as He called men to enter it. The apostolic conception is the same : " And the Lord added to the Church, day by day, those that were being saved." ‡

THE CHURCH'S AIM SPIRITUAL.

The purpose of the Church was not ethical, but religious ; not philanthropic but spiritual. Its chief business was not to go about social reform, but to effect the regeneration of the inner life. It was to deal not primarily with the body, but

* Matthew xvi. 18. † Mark xvi. 16. ‡ Acts ii. 47.

the soul. Its aim was to eradicate sin, not to heal sickness. From this new Christian life, recreated in the image of Christ, there would issue, as a secondary but inevitable result, the leaven of social righteousness and the streams of beneficence and pity in unwonted vitality and power. With this thought in view Ignatius writes: "A Christian has not power over himself, but must always be ready for the service of the Church." * The service of physical want and needs was but to be instrumental to the service and healing of the spirit. The bodily help was to be an avenue through which the soul could be reached and turned toward the heavenly goal.

That this secondary result was most effectually reached by the Church holding fast to religion and the conversion and saving of the soul as her prime duty is shown by such emphatic testimonies as that which Gibbon in the "Decline and Fall of the Roman Empire" bears to the blessed change which the spirit of Christianity wrought in the hard, pitiless and selfish Pagan world. The Gospel that transformed the soul made it an agent of "love in the service of those who suffer."

* "Epistle to Polycarp," chap. vii.

NECESSITY OF THE CHURCH.

This was the view of the Church held by the apostolic fathers. They believe its purpose is to convert and save men, and through this means to reform and uplift society. And if it ever occurs to them that enlightened men can secure this salvation out of the Church they do not state it. Their position is that the Church is Christ's mystical Body, and that they who wish to share His redemptive power must be members of that mystical Body. Hermas thus likens the Church to a tower builded on the earth; the saved are all gathered into it, the unsaved remain without. His words are: " If you desire to enter into a city and the city is surrounded by a wall and has but one gate, can you enter into that city save through its gate? So, in like manner, a man cannot otherwise enter into the kingdom of God." * This corresponds to the rule of Augustine: " He who has not the Church for his mother cannot have God for his Father." Of course, both are treating of the rule; exceptions belong to the providence and mercy of God. It is assumed that Christ instituted the Church to propagate His gospel. Christianity and churchliness are deemed in-

* " The Shepherd," Book III., " Similitude," chap. xii.

separable. That one should share in the salvation provided for a lost world and yet not confess Christ, not enter the visible kingdom of God, not join with the faithful in the holy mysteries of the sacraments, was to the fathers inconceivable. In no later period of christian history were the lines more sharply drawn between the Church and the world, between confessors and non-confessors.

CHRISTIAN UNITY.

Unity is a prime trait of the Church. The holy Church universal is *one*. It was to have "one body, one Spirit, one Lord, one faith, one baptism, one hope," * the world over. In this it was to be a contrast to earthly kingdoms. Their divisions, strifes and discords, were to be unknown in this blessed spiritual unity. There is nothing, accordingly, that the apostolic fathers so deplore and seek to repress as schisms of any kind between christian brethren. Thus Ignatius: "If any man follow him that makes a schism in the Church, he shall not inherit the kingdom of God." † Again: "Live in unblamable unity, that you may always enjoy communion with God." ‡ Clement: "Ye, there-

* Ephesians iv. 4, 5.   † Epistle to Philadelphians, chap. iii.
‡ Epistle to Ephesians, chap. iv.

fore, who laid the foundation of this schism repent, bending the knees of your hearts." * The idea of churches with divers confessions, rearing ecclesiastical bars, excluding from mutual inter-fellowship, would have been considered an un-christian rending of the body of Christ. " These early testimonies," says Canon Westcott, " prove that christianity was *catholic* from the very first, uniting a variety of forms in one faith. They show that the great facts of the Gospel narrative and the substance of the Apostolic Epistles formed the basis and molded the expression of the common creed." †

Accordingly an open door awaited the members of any one congregation when they passed to that of another. And the various churches interchanged letters for the mutual strengthening of faith and for cementing still more strongly the close bonds of christian unity. " The designation of the universal Christian Church as Catholic, dates from the time of Irenæus (130 A. D.), that is, from the beginning of the second part of our first period. This name characterizes the Church as the one universally spread and recognized from the time of the

* First Epistle, chap. lvii.
† " History of the Canon," p. 55.

apostles, and so stigmatizes every opposition to the one Church that alone stands as the sure foundation of Holy Scripture and pure apostolic tradition, as belonging to particularistic, heretical and schismatical sects." *

AUTHORITY.

A further note of the Church was authority. The liberal Roman Catholic Loisy is right when he asks, What is a "kingdom" without authority? † No kingdom or institution can exist, can have a consistent historical development, or stand for anything definite, without a constraining and regulative authority. So our Lord recognizes the authority of the Church: "Tell it to the Church, and if he neglect to hear the Church let him be unto thee a heathen and a publican." ‡ This authority, after the Lord's ascension, was lodged with the apostles. They exercised supreme rule over the Church. In Acts xv. we find the apostles co-operating in this rule with the whole Church, so that their decree goes out, "The apostles and elders and brethren send greeting," etc. Later, Paul speaks of it as

* "Church History," Kurtz, Vol. I., p. 72.
† "The Gospel and the Church," p. 147.
‡ Matthew xviii. 17.

THE HOLY CHRISTIAN CHURCH. 95

issuing from the Presbytery. * And, at a still later period, as the Church spread through many lands, General Councils, representative of the whole christian community, were to settle vexed and disturbing questions. In the era we are describing, although there was no constituted court, yet the idea of authority was fully acknowledged. Thus writes Hermas: "The Church is the city of God with its own laws." † Of these laws the bishop or pastor of each congregation was the representative. And so influential was the spirit of Christ and the teaching of the apostles, that this authority was found effectual for preserving purity of doctrine and the peace of the Church.

This, the apostolic conception of the Church, is that taught in these writings of the next generation. The visible form of the spiritual kingdom of God, holy, one, universal, authoritative, instituted by Christ, founded by the Holy Ghost on the day of Pentecost, and the instrument of the Holy Ghost for the application of the means of grace to the conversion of souls and to the doing the work of God in the world, until the whole earth should be

* 1 Timothy iv., 14.
† "Similitude," I., 1, 3, 9.

redeemed from the reign of darkness and translated into the kingdom of light.

This note of authority has, in many parts of the modern Church, been largely lost. To break away from allegiance to Christ, to Scriptures and to creed, and to preach a doctrine of liberty, recognizing alone the autonomy of the human conscience, is a current tendency. "Religion itself," writes Professor Woodberry, "so far as the general thought of nineteenth century civilization is concerned, has suffered a diminution of authority, and consequently the spiritual life of man has filled a less prominent part in the eyes of these generations." * There is an authority of science, an authority of reason, and no less an authority of faith. Christ was authority over the mind for truth, as well as an example for conduct. The Church is the kingdom in which He rules, and it is only when she comes to men in His name and with His divine and irresistible authority, that men will heed her message. "In this loyalty to the gospel lies the hope of the Church. Outside of it is suicidal division." †

* "Makers of Literature," p. 147.
† "The Church and the Changing Order," Professor Shailer Matthews, p. 89.

CHAPTER XIII.

CHURCH GOVERNMENT AND POLITY.

THE conception of the Church we here see prevailing is an intensely spiritual one. Yet, as there must be an outward organization, and as for that authority and laws are essential, the question arises, what shall this form be? Is there one prescribed in the New Testament? We find there no definite model fixed, and but the faintest features outlined. This evidently means that the particular form of church organization was a matter of freedom to be determined by the exigencies of time and occasion.

Provided, then, that the pure faith be retained, one form of government, adapted to the spirit of a people, or to the particular needs of an age, is just as legitimate as any other, and should prove no bar to inter-christian fellowship. This is the view of the constitution of the Church which Luther took, as learned from Scripture, and as justified by the excesses and oppression to which the Roman Catholic view had led. That conception of the Church as a great material organization, with its central seat in Rome, and its authority absolute and infallible, extending over all the churches to the minutest detail, is thus set forth by Loisy: "The Church had to find for herself a government or cease to exist; but government in a church, one and universal, is inconceivable without a central authority. A central ideal, with no real power as conceived by Cyprian, would have been useless. Particular councils could not have had sufficient prestige; General Councils could never have been anything but a tribunal for extraordinary occasions, and experience showed that these assemblies had many great inconveniences. The tribunal, before which all more important cases should naturally come, by which all conflicts should be finally decided, could be only that Church, the most apostolic of all, holding the traditions of Peter and Paul, whose chiefs did not hesitate to call themselves successors of the Prince of the Apostles." *

THE CHURCH NOT A HIERARCHY.

But this hierarchical scheme receives no countenance in the literature of our Patristic age. These

---

* "The Gospel and the Church," p. 160.

CHURCH GOVERNMENT AND POLITY. 99

writers know nothing of it as an historical fact, and their statements positively exclude its existence. The author of the Didache knows of no primacy of Peter. "The Epistle of Ignatius to the Romans is utterly inconsistent with any conception on his part that Rome was the see and residence of a bishop holding any other than fraternal relations with himself." * Not in all the writers of this first century is there an intimation that Peter had ever been Bishop of Rome. In their references to the individual apostles, Paul is ever referred to in the highest terms as the second founder of Christianity. Ignatius is the first father to use the phrase Catholic Church, but in so characterizing it he defines it to be " wherever Christ is," making no reference to a primacy of St. Peter. Moreover, in their constant references to the Church we find only a spiritual conception of it, with Jesus Christ as its Head, which consists alone with a spiritual authority and not with the idea of a temporal sceptre wielded by the Roman, or any other pontificate.

For example, Barnabas, after showing that the material temple at Jerusalem with its hierarchical

* Bishop A. Cleveland Coxe, "The Anti-Nicene Fathers," Vol. I., p. 46.

system has been superseded by the Christian Church, comments: "Is there, then, still a temple of God? Such a temple does exist. Learn, then, how it is built in the name of the Lord. Before we believed, our heart was corrupt, as being indeed like a temple made with hands. But, having received the forgiveness of sins, we have become new creatures. Wherefore, in our habitation God truly dwells in us." * Man thus becomes the dwelling of God and the Church a spiritual temple, in which the glory of Christ, the invisible King, manifests itself in the hearts of believing members. Thus a thoroughly spiritual idea of religion, of the Church as a spiritual kingdom, and of worship, not as a round of external rites and duties, but as a service of heart and life, permeates these writings.

The momentous transformation in the idea of the Church took place in the next century under Cyprian. The evangelical definition of the Church is superseded by the Roman Catholic. The Church is no longer essentially the assembly of believers and saints, nor an object of faith, but a visible body, controlled by divinely-authorized ecclesiastical law. The chief claim made for this view, viz.:

* Epistle, chap. xvi.

that it has the warrant of history and tradition, is positively negatived by the undeniable fact that such a tradition was non-existent during this sub-apostolic era and for nearly two centuries after Christ. The primitive tradition, then, is decisively against it.

The theory and practice disclosed here teach, therefore, that such polity and government as are necessary for the administration of the Church as a visible organization, are relegated to the freedom of Christendom. And this principle, making the Church capable of adaptability to all varieties of race and temperament, to either republican or monarchical forms of government, and to all the changing conditions of history, is the one best calculated for an institution that is to have the mark of universality.

CHAPTER XIV.

THE CHRISTIAN MINISTRY.

The New Testament abrogated the priestly hierarchy of the Old Testament. In the new spiritual kingdom of God there was to be no separate priestly order. There is under the Christian dispensation an universal priesthood. Every man is his own priest and need not go to a distinct class to whom divine grace is bound alone. Nevertheless, all things must be done in order. Each individual must be willing to transfer the exercise of his right to one who represents him in the necessary ministrations of the Church. This necessitates the ministry, —not as an order but as an office. It is charged with the oversight of the Church. This office is of divine institution. At first Christ gave an immediate call to the twelve, named apostles. They founded churches and set ministers over them. Thus the institution of the ministerial office was directly divine. The apostolic fathers ever so considered it. Thus Ignatius: "Bishops are by the will of Christ."* Clement: "Both these appointments,

* Epistle to Ephesians, chap. ii.

then [of officers of the Church], were made in an orderly way according to the will of God." *

NO MINISTERIAL ORDERS.

The three orders in the ministry,—bishop, priest and deacon,—as claimed by high church systems, find no warrant here. The term "priest" is unused by the fathers. The Christian minister is not a priest in the Old Testament sense. He does not stand in the holy place as a mediator between God and man offering sacrifice. That has been accomplished by the one great High Priest, Jesus Christ, "who now once in the end of the world hath appeared to put away sin by the sacrifice of Himself." †

Polycarp, in writing his Epistle to the Philippians, begins: "Polycarp and the presbyters [ministers] with him [at Smyrna], to the Church of God sojourning at Philippi." Further on in the epistle he urges the Philippians to be "subject to their presbyters and deacons." This language is inconceivable had there been a bishop of a distinct and superior order, set over the presbyters at Philippi. Evidently there were but the presbyters,

* Epistle, " Order of Ministers in the Church," chap. xlii.
† Hebrews ix. 26.

and the deacons, as a divinely-appointed office to aid the ministry, as instituted by the apostles (Acts vi. 3). So Clement, St. Paul's co-laborer: "The apostles, having first proved them by the Spirit, appointed bishops [used in the New Testament and the early Patristic writings as a synonym of presbyter, just as we say minister, pastor or clergyman, denoting the same office] and deacons of those who should afterward believe." * The Church, then, as we find it organized, when the apostles had passed away, was under the supervision of but two classes of officers—the bishop or presbyter, *i. e.*, the minister—and the deacon, *i. e.*, the diaconate.

Deaconesses were also appointed. The office of the diaconate was at first instituted especially as a ministry of mercy. Later it came to be regarded as a subordinate order of clergy, whose chief duty it was to aid the minister in public worship. The office of the deaconess was that of care for the sick and suffering. According to the "Apostolic Constitutions" the female diaconate arose from the many necessities of the Church connected with works of charity and relief, especially among women, which such female officials were more es-

* Epistle, "Order of Ministers in the Church," chap. xlii.

pecially fitted to discharge. Besides these there were no other regular Church offices. The three orders—bishop, presbyter, and deacon—are an unsupported fiction.

APOSTOLICAL SUCCESSION.

The apostolical succession falls with that of clerical orders. The claim that the apostles appointed the episcopate as the succession to the apostolate, clothed with its powers and with that of a perpetual succession, and that no other church constitution is legitimate—a tremendous claim, indeed—is without historical support. It is admitted that it is not authorized in Scripture, and hence, if authorized at all, must have been given by the apostles through tradition to our fathers of the ensuing generation and by them transmitted to following times. But they are unaware of such a succession. With the ministerial office ever in their minds and hearts and upon their pens, not a suggestion that they know of it escapes them. Ignatius, with all his tendencies to exalt so extremely the clergy, is yet ignorant of it.

Harnack is justified in saying: " Ignatius knew nothing about the apostolic succession, (the bishop

is the representative of God unto His own church), and neither did Clement, and even the basal document of the Apostolical Constitutions is silent." *
The learned Bishop Lightfoot, himself so honored a representative of the Church of England, is equally positive. Quoting Ignatius in the Epistle to the Magnesians, chap. vi.: "If the bishop occupies the place of God, or of Jesus Christ, the presbyters are as the apostles, or the council of God," the bishop comments: "This comparison shows how widely the idea of the episcopate differed from the later conception, when it had been formulated in the doctrine of the apostolical succession. The presbyters, *not the bishops*, are here the representatives of the apostles. Of a diocese, properly so called, there is no trace." † And again he writes of Clement: "Not only have we no traces of a bishop of bishops, but even the very existence of a bishop at Rome itself could nowhere be gathered from this epistle of Clement. We find ἐπισκοπος still used as a synonym for πρεσβύτερος as it is in the New Testatment. It should be remembered

* "History of Dogma," p. 96.
† "Apostolic Fathers, Epistles of St. Ignatius," Vol. I., p. 397.

THE CHRISTIAN MINISTRY. 107

that when Clement wrote this epistle, the last of the twelve apostles [John], if the best ancient tradition may be credited, was still living, the center of a body of Christian disciples, at Ephesus." *

ORIGIN OF THE EPISCOPAL FICTION.

How, then, did it come about that this theory should become the foundation upon which was reared the hierarchical system destined to play so vast and harmful a part in the history of the Church of Christ? As Christianity spread and churches multiplied and there were many ministers in a city or district, a presbytery was formed for mutual deliberation and strength. Over this body a president was elected. At first he was only *primus inter pares*, the first among equals, simply a leader of his brethren. By degrees he grew in prominence and power. In the severe persecutions it was almost absolutely necessary that all power be concentrated in his hands.

And finally a reason was discovered for his not surrendering it. For a century later we find it strongly championed by Irenæus, who writes: " The charisma of truth depends upon the office of the

* Ibid., Vol. I., p. 352.

bishops, which rests upon the apostolic succession." It originated in the Western Church, but was much later in gaining recognition in the Orient, although at the time of Origen it began to appear at Alexandria. Chrysostom, in the fourth century, protests: "Let the bishops know that they are greater by custom than by any real appointment of Christ." And Jerome, the renowned author of the Vulgate —the Bible of the Christian world for a thousand years—says: "Among the primitive fathers, presbyters and bishops were the very same, but, little by little, all the authority was concentrated in the bishop." That the apostolical succession had this origin, Bishop Lightfoot declares thus: "The episcopate was formed, not out of the apostolic order, but out of the presbyterate, and the title, which originally was common to all, came at length to be appropriated to the chief among them." This original identity of presbyter and bishop is not only insisted on by Lutherans, Presbyterians, Congregationalists, Reformed, Methodists, Baptists, etc., but it is freely admitted by the foremost scholars of the Church of England, as Whitby, Bloomfield, Conybeare, Howson, Alford, Ellicott, Lightfoot, etc., etc.

The episcopate, as an office of the Church, may

be of the utmost administrative value, most efficient for wise oversight and a stronghold of Christian unity. But, as grounded upon a succession of the apostolate, it is distinctly anti-Scriptural, anti-Patristic, Romish, exclusive, bigoted and charged with dangerous hierarchical potencies. The only legitimate apostolic succession is the succession of the apostolic faith. The idea still prevalent in this primitive era is, then, the Scriptural one that the ministry is not a priestly caste with sacerdotal functions, nor a succession to the apostolate through whom alone grace is transmitted, but an office instituted by Christ. "Pastors are stewards of the mysteries of God" and shepherds for the care of souls.

THE EPISCOPATE AS AN OFFICE.

Respecting the episcopate, looked upon not as an order but as an office of the Church, the notable fact that it came at so early a period into universal prevalence and has so flourished in large parts of the Church to the present time, is undeniably of the greatest significance. Neander declares that "the triumph of the episcopal system undoubtedly promoted the unity, order and tranquillity of the churches," * at a time when such united action was necessary to preserve their very existence. An office in the Church of such venerable history and bringing such efficient vigor to the administration of the Church, and so successful in the churches using it to-day, may well challenge our regard. It provides a supervision by a wise and experienced head, which pastors and congregations so often need. The episcopate is probably the wisest form of the Christian ministry.

As to the manner of calling ministers, they were appointed by the bishops or presbytery, with the consent and approval of the congregation. "The first presbyters were chosen directly by the apostles (Titus i. 5 compared with Acts xiv. 23), while in the times immediately succeeding they were appointed by those who, even at this date, were already styled bishops, not, however, without the assent and concurrence of the whole laity." † Clement: "We are of opinion that those appointed by the apostles, or afterwards by other eminent men, *with the consent of the whole Church*, who

---

* "History of the Christian Religion and Church," Vol. I., p. 193.

† "Christian Antiquities," sec. viii., p. 25, Guericke.

have blamelessly served the flock of Christ, cannot be justly dismissed from the ministry." * The Didache states this rule [as apostolic] : " Appoint (or elect), therefore, for yourselves, bishops and deacons, worthy of the Lord, men meek and not lovers of money, and truthful and proved." †

THE MINISTERIAL CALL AND ORDINATION.

The call to, or choice for, the ministry comes, then, from the Church, either through the individual congregation, or representatively through the Presbytery or Synod. Originally, the presbyters were chosen and ordained by the laying on of hands, either by an individual apostle, or by the college of presbyters, as St. Paul says to Timothy : " Neglect not the gift that is in thee, which was given thee by prophecy, with the laying on of the hands of the presbytery." ‡ Although the congregation was consulted and final action only taken with its approval, yet the original choice was made by an apostle or a body representative of the whole Church. Paul sends Titus to " ordain elders in every city," and

* Epistle, chap. xliv.
† " Bishops and Deacons," chap. xv.
‡ 1 Tim. iv. 14.

this not only in the founding of new congregations, but also in the case of congregations that had already been organized. There is no instance in the New Testament where a congregation makes an original selection for itself of its pastor. But the choice, which it may ratify or reject, comes from a higher source, representative of the authority of the whole Church. This is necessary, also, because an individual congregation is not competent to pass upon the theological attainments requisite for one to fill worthily the ministerial office. Hence, we find no Scripture precedent for that modern laxity which would leave the choice wholly to the congregation.

The induction into the office was, by the rite of ordination, conferred by the laying on of hands, with the prayers of the congregation. The Scriptures attribute a special "gift of God which is in thee by the putting on of my hands"* to ordination, a gift or grace which is distinct from the grace conferred in the sacraments. That ordination need not be repeated, like installation into the pastorate of an individual congregation, is significant of the fact that it represents an authority not emanating di-

* 2 Tim. i. 6.

rectly from the individual congregation, but conferred by the whole Church representatively.

THE MINISTERIAL OFFICE.

The sphere of the ministry is preaching the word, administering the sacraments, and the exercise of the power of the keys—*i. e.*, the declaration of the remission or retention of sins, to the believing or unbelieving, as authorized by the gospel (John xx. 23). Sacramental grace is not validated by the ministry, but by the power of the word.

The Lutheran theologian and acute thinker, Martensen, says: " Though we do not depreciate priestly ordination, we do not rank it with the sacraments—Baptism and the Lord's Supper—far less place it above these. This is the very secret *falsum* of a hierarchy, that it makes ordination in reality the chief sacrament, for the efficacy of all the other sacraments depends upon this, that the priest has been ordained ; so that the priesthood actually becomes the constituent and sustaining principle of the Church. The evangelical Church, on the contrary, maintains most distinctly that it is not ordination that gives the sacraments their efficacy, but the word and appointment of God alone." *

* " Christian Dogmatics," p. 448.

Still, the legitimate administration of the sacraments, as a matter of order, pertains to the ministerial office. "Let that alone," says Ignatius, "be deemed a legitimate Eucharist, which is administered by the bishop. It is not lawful without the bishop to baptize—so that everything that is done may be valid." * "They also render to you the service of prophets and teachers,"† says the Didache. All that embraces the guidance and care of souls belongs to the office of the holy ministry.

* Epistle to the Smyrnaeans, chap. viii.
† "Bishops and Deacons," chap. xv.

CHAPTER XV.

AUTHORITY OF CHURCH AND MINISTRY.

HOLDING these simple, non-priestly, evangelical beliefs as to the ministry does not prevent the fathers from according to the office a legitimate authority. While mediately it is given through the Church, it comes immediately from the Holy Ghost, and is therefore of divine institution and authority. The authority of the minister was not temporal but spiritual, but in that sphere he was supreme. He was looked upon as the representative of God, clothed with the power of the Word.

Pastors were, therefore, not only to be loved, but to be obeyed. Leaders and rulers by divine investiture, their judgment is decisive, and submission to it, though voluntary, is a Christian duty. And, as "holiness," in the words of Amiel, "is the chief authority of the ministry," their lives of sacrifice and saintliness, in this testing age, strengthened this sentiment of reverence. Ignatius writes: "I exhort you to do all things with a divine harmony, while your bishop presides in the place of God, and your presbyters in the place of the assembly of the apostles, along with your deacons, who are intrusted with the ministry of Jesus Christ." * In like manner he says: "Let all reverence the deacons as an appointment of Jesus Christ, and the bishop as Jesus Christ, and the presbyters as the Sanhedrin of God and assembly of the apostles." †

Yet, strong as is this language, and certainly an advance upon Clement and Hermas, it is not meant that bishops, were of apostolical appointment any more than presbyters and deacons. It is simply a strong affirmation of the spiritual authority of the leaders of the Church, as holding their appointment from Jesus Christ, and representative of Him as the Church's head. Thus writes Professor Uhlhorn: "Ignatius knows nothing about an apostolical establishment of an episcopate, nor does he connect it with those ideas of a priesthood which afterward were borrowed from the Old Testament. The episcopate is to him an office in the congregation, not an office in the Church. The bishop is to him not the successor of the apostles, nor is he the bearer of the doctrinal tradition."

---

* Epistle to Magnesians, chap. vi.
† Epistle to Trallians, chap. iii.

AUTHORITY A NECESSITY.

But the ministry stands for order, for purity of doctrine, and for discipline, which are a necessity, however voluntary be membership in a society. So Ignatius writes: "Let all things, therefore, be done by you with good order in Christ. Let the laity be subject to the deacons; the deacons to the presbyters; the presbyters to the bishop; the bishop to Christ, even as He is to the Father."* While the essential equality of the laity is conceded, yet when once they have placed their representative in the ministerial office, and while he has not been removed, which right Clement asserts for the congregation, his spiritual authority is to be deferred to. He is to be truly leader, guide and head.

Beyond question, there is a legitimate authority vested in the Church for efficient administration. Without this there is no means for securing its efficiency or for maintaining its identity, or for preserving its very existence. This authority the Church has exercised to decide the limits of the canon of Holy Scripture. And nothing was more absolutely essential to Christendom. But for this

* Epistle to the Smyrnaeans, chap. ix.

believers could not for ages have rested in the possession of the pure and uncorrupted word of God.

GENERAL COUNCILS.

Similar authority has established the ecumenical creeds, as guardians of the foundation truth of the divinity of Christ, and the scriptural doctrines of sin, grace and redemption. As the ministry has been locally authoritative for the individual congregations, so supreme questions of doctrine have been settled by authority of General Councils, representing the whole Church.

Luther justly challenged the infallibility of even these councils and showed how in many cases they had erred. As in the case of civil government, the right of revolution inheres to the Church and was exercised in the Reformation to the rescue of that greatest boon, religious freedom. But such exceptional crises do not mean that the Church is to be without legitimate and regular authority or that every member shall believe and do that which is "right in his own eyes." The Church has authority by the Word of God to set up tests of a pure confession, to exclude heretics and to discipline unworthy members. Christ could have meant no less than this when He gave into her hands "the power of the keys."

DANGERS OF INDIVIDUALISM.

Liberal as was Emerson, he saw the danger to which Protestantism was here exposed, and wrote: "Now men fall abroad—want polarity—suffer in character and intellect. Luther would cut off his right hand sooner than write theses against the Pope, if he suspected that he was bringing on with all his might the pale negations of Boston Unitarianism. To a self-denying, ardent Church has succeeded a cold, intellectual race, who analyze the prayer and psalm of their forefathers, and reject every yoke of authority and custom with a petulance unprecedented. It is a mark of probity to declare how little you believe, and we have punctuality for faith and good taste for character." It is well for Protestantism to heed this warning and to take care that liberty be not caricatured into license, and that the right of private judgment be not made a shield for lawless excess.

While we are thankful to escape that domination, which in the Roman Church holds in its grip freedom of conscience, represses the spirit of inquiry and exorcises scientific progress, let us guard against the dangers of the opposite extreme. To allow heresies to poison her very vitals, to tolerate assaults upon her foundations, to permit all manner of breaches in her unity, is certainly an abnegation of that authority which she has received from her Lord and without the exercise of which no kingdom, human or divine, temporal or spiritual, can exist.

If Neander holds that the unquestioned authority of the Church, in the third and fourth centuries, " undoubtedly promoted order, unity and tranquillity," in a time when persecution and the greatest dangers threatened Christendom with destruction, and if it was the means of bringing the Church safely through this trying period, none the less is a reasonable degree of authority needed to rescue the Church from the perils which confront it in this modern time.

As a sign of healthful reaction amid the cries in the air for an utterly unregulated license of opinion over against an ordered faith, one is pleased to read such words as these, lately written : " The question of the ultimate authority for mankind is the greatest of all questions which meet the West, since the

Catholic Church lost its place in the sixteenth century and since criticism no longer allows the Bible to occupy that place. Yet the gospel of the future must come with the note of authority, and that note must sound in whatever is the supreme utterance of the Church, in polity, pulpit or creed. The Church can never part with the tone of authority, nor with the claim that, however it may be defined, the authority of its message is supreme. That is the very genius of evangelical religion." *

* "Positive Preaching and Modern Mind," Forsyth, p. 41.

CHAPTER XVI.

CHRISTIANITY AND THE SUPERNATURAL—MIRACLES AND THE RESURRECTION.

THREE views of the supernatural are prevalent in present thinking. One denies it altogether. Miracles have never occurred. No break in the uniformity of nature has ever taken place. There is no proof, or, as Hume put it, there can be no proof to validate a divine extraordinary intervention. As representative of this attitude, a late review in the *Outlook* of Archbishop French's work on the miracles of our Lord, says: " Since His time the progress of learning has carried the discussion of *miracles* to a further point than He rested at. The wonderful works of Jesus in healing disease, treated in this volume as miraculous, are not so regarded by modern psychologists." Sabatier thus frankly states this position: "The modern historian never presupposes a miracle. However imposing may be the destinies of the Church, its birth, its development, its triumphs and its reverses are none the less a series of phenomena, interlinked and conditioned by the circumstances of time and place, like all other historic phenomena. If miracle is found neither in the circumstances nor the progress of the history, in which have met and mingled all the social forces of two thousand years, why should it have occurred at the beginning?"* So Professor Foster, of Chicago University, declares, with the indorsement of that body, in his recent book on The Finality of the Christian Religion, that "a miracle cannot be admitted." According to this view either Christ must have played upon the superstitious weakness of invalids, or what He professed to be "wonderful works" were wrought by mental suggestion, telepathy, or some other form of pyschotherapy.

A second view removes the bar between the natural and supernatural. One is but a development of the other. They are obverse and transverse sides of the same thing. As says Dr. Whiton: "The natural is the outwardness of the supernatural; the supernatural is the inwardness of the natural." When our perception reaches a larger range we will see that the forces of nature have the capacity of the supernatural and merge into it. All

* "Religions of Authority and of the Spirit," p. 19.

the wonders, therefore, claiming to have been wrought by Christ were simply natural, and may be reproduced by some advanced psychologist.

The reply to this is that supernatural and natural stand for two thoughts, which do not supplement, but exclude each other. The natural is the exercise of ordinary, the supernatural of extraordinary power. The natural is uniform, the supernatural is exceptional. The natural is traceable to second causes, the supernatural is unaccountable by any second cause. Certainly two separate, distinct ideas are embraced here, and if language is to be the organ of intelligible thought, then these diverse ideas cannot better be differentiated than by the diverse terms, natural and supernatural.

The third view is the historic Christian one, affirming the reality of the supernatural.

FUNDAMENTAL NATURE OF THE CONTROVERSY.

The question involved is fundamental. It lies at the very heart of religion. All religions have claimed supernatural sanction. And this because without such sanction they are not religions but philosophies. They are merely subjective guesses, blind gropings after God. A *religion* unveils the unseen, gives sight of the invisible, makes known objective facts as to the immaterial sphere, instead of fancies. It answers those questions which the natural reason finds unanswerable. That is, it must be a *revelation*. And a revelation cannot be natural, for that is a self-contradiction in terms. "What kind of a revelation would that be," asks Lessing, "which reveals nothing?" Unless it unveils that which is beyond the reach of our natural powers, it can give us no more than the great Pagan thinkers attained, of whom Luthardt writes: "A strain of inconsolable lament, arising from despair as to future existence, runs through all their great literatures." *

THE PATRISTIC TEACHING.

On this far-reaching problem, there is no doubt as to the position of our Patristic authors. They accept Christianity as not only having features of the supernatural, but as based upon it. This is indisputable from a perusal of their works. The references to the supernatural constitute the warp and woof of their utterances. "The mysteries of the gospel," is an ever-recurrent phrase.

* "Fundamental Truths of Christianity," p. 317.

First of all, they regard Christ as a supernatural personality. He is supernatural in his *pre-existence*. Other men's lives begun in natural birth, but He "pre-existed eternally."* His *nativity* was supernatural. Other beings have a human father and mother, but "Christ was begotten by the Father before all ages, but was afterwards born of the Virgin Mary without any intercourse with man." † The virginity of Mary, the nativity, and the sacrificial death of Christ, are called the three cardinal mysteries. "God the Word," says Barnabas, "was truly born of a virgin."

The *Person* of Christ was a mystery. "Jesus, who was manifested by type and in the flesh, is not the Son of man, but the Son of God." ‡ He is the God-Man, the divine and human blended in His mysterious person.

His life was supernatural in its *sinlessness*. This unique feature set Him apart from all others of natural birth, into whose being passed the inevitable stain of sin. His *words* were supernatural. He spoke as never man spake. He revealed the invisible, for it was His pre-existent home. "He

---

* Ignatius to the Magnesians, chap. xi.
† Ibid.   ‡ Epistle of Barnabas, chap. xii.

brought immortality to light." He spoke as familiarly of heaven as of earth.

He was invested with supernatural *powers*. He is the Teacher who "spoke and it was done." All the main constituents of His life rose above the natural. Writes Ignatius : " He lived a sinless life, and healed every kind of sickness and disease among the people, and wrought signs and wonders for the benefit of men. He made known the one and only true God. He endured the cross, died and rose again, and ascended into the heavens, and is set down at the right hand of God, and shall come at the end of the world with His Father's glory, to judge the living and the dead." *

They believed the *Christian life* itself to be a supernatural one. It was a second birth, a spiritual creation, a new and heavenly beginning wrought by the Holy Spirit. And its continuance was by a mystical union with Christ, through the indwelling of the Holy Spirit, who made of the soul and body a spiritual temple.

They perceived a supernatural aspect in the *Atonement*. In it Christ, sinless, identified Himself with sinful humanity, and, as its representative,

* Epistle to the Magnesians, chap. xi.

was bruised in its stead, dying, the just for the unjust, in contravention of a natural equity.

They teach that the *sacraments* have a supernatural side. In both baptism and the Lord's Supper, there are not alone present the natural constituents, water, and bread and wine, but a supernatural grace, sacramentally united with these earthly agents.

And, finally, they hold that the *records* of all the events and teachings and doctrines constituting this revelation have more than a natural authority. They regard them as divinely true, quoting them not as ordinary human writings, but as the "Sacred Scriptures," and not merely as uninspired productions, but as the word of God, indicted by the Holy Ghost.

Now, as these fathers had minds as we, intuitively suspicious of every cause that puts forth claims to the supernatural, and, as living so near the time, they could find eye-witnesses and first-hand testimony, it cannot be doubted that they searchingly investigated the evidence for these remarkable pretensions. And the result was that they were so convinced by indubitable proofs, that they risked upon the reality of them their reputations, their temporal well-being, their lives and the everlasting welfare of their souls.

And, in presenting the new religion for the conversion of Jews and Gentiles, they do not hide or repress these supernatural characteristics, but keep them in the very forefront as the salient truths of their message. For, though they well knew that they will be be but "foolishness" to the philosophical Greek mind, and a "stumbling-block" to Jewish prejudice, they, on the other hand, are fully assured that it is just in these exceptional marks that Christianity attests itself "the power of God, and the wisdom of God." * To be a Christian one must first of all bow his reason to these divine mysteries. For, says Ignatius, "If anyone praises the creation, but calls the incarnation merely an appearance, he hath denied the faith." †

* 1 Cor. i. 24.   † Epistle to Philippians, chap. vi.

CHAPTER XVII.

THE APOSTOLIC FATHERS AND CURRENT VIEWS AS TO THE SUPERNATURAL.

THE point here discussed is a living and crucial one to-day. The last century has been marked by the attack of one school after another upon the supernatural in revealed religion. It cannot be denied that the New Testament accounts of Christianity represent its origin as interwoven with supernatural events. For example, the evangelists record thirty-three miracles wrought by the Saviour, and adding to these the miraculous features of the birth narrative, and those attendant upon the crucifixion, and those crowned by the greatest of all, the resurrection, it can be seen how large a part of the brief biographies is occupied by the supernatural element.

This shows the impossibility of representing these miraculous characteristics as but the scaffolding of Christianity, which, the edifice completed, can be thrown away. "Contrariwise," as Professor W. H. Green has said, "our religion is an historical religion based on a series of redemptive acts. And to cast doubt on the reality of the historical occurrences is to cast doubt on the reality of that religion which they embodied."

EVOLUTION OR REVELATION OF THE SCRIPTURES.

The gist of much of modern Biblical criticism is to account for the origin of the Old Testament by a process of evolution. Only natural factors and forces were operative in the process by which the various books of the Old Testament grew. Their contents did not come down from God, but rose up by degrees from the mental laboratories and varied experiences of the nation and its authors. "In reality," as Kuenen openly acknowledges, "the 'newer criticism' has a standpoint which includes among other claims that the religion of the Old Testament is one of the most important religions; nothing less, but nothing more."

Comparing these views with the Old Testament itself we see them to be altogether irreconcilable. The Old Testament claims at every step of the history of Israel a divine intervention. The whole book is a great supernatural stage in which God is ever, not through secondary natural causes, but directly, appearing on the scene. He calls Abraham. He gives the commandments in His own handwriting to Moses. He works signs and wonders to sanction His word, to deliver His chosen people and to advance His divine purpose.

From first to last, the volume claims a distinction from all other volumes on the ground that it is a record of a series of divine redemptive acts, and that its contents sprang not from the natural reason, but that, as St. Peter says, "The prophecy came not in old time by the will of man, but holy men of old spake as they were moved by the Holy Ghost." * If, then, it really emanated but as other books, and if all these pretended divine revelations and superhuman wonders were but the cunning devices of the writers, could a more palpable fraud than this be perpetrated—all the worse when done in the holy name of religion!

Well does Bishop Ellicott say: "We are beginning to realize the gravity of the Old Testament controversy. The traditional views are being re-examined under the light of modern discoveries, and efforts are being made to put in contrast that inspired and trustworthy record of the past, bearing

* Second Epistle, ii. 21.

the name of the Old Testament and sealed with a belief of more than two thousand years in its genuineness and integrity, with that strange conglomerate of myth, legend, fabrication, idealized narrative, falsified history, dramatized fable and after-event prophecy, to which modern critical analysis has sought to reduce that which the Church, day by day, calls the most Holy Word of Almighty God." *

The same critical alembic is to be applied to the New Testament. The motive that has impelled many modern students of our Lord's life has been their hope and endeavor to account for Christ on the basis of a purely natural development, to find the secret of His power in the conditions of His individuality and age, and to explain His person and His works in the terms of the laws of psychological and historical evolution. They have found no more eloquent interpreter than Renan. " Let us place, then, at the summit of human greatness the person of Jesus. Humanity presents in its totality an assemblage of low beings, selfish, superior to the animal only in the single particular that its selfishness is more reflective. Still, from the midst of this uniform depravity, pillars rise toward the sky

* "Christus Comprobator," chap. ii., pp. 43, 44.

and testify to a nobler destiny. Jesus is the highest of these pillars that show to man whence he comes and whither he ought to tend. In Him was concentrated all that is good and elevated in our nature." * Yet this splendid panegyric follows a passage expressly denying anything superhuman in Christ's being.

What, then, are these claimed results of modern scholarship? One writer sums them up thus: "A pantheistic god instead of a personal God. A human saviour instead of a divine Saviour. Infallible scholarship instead of an infallible Bible. Reformation instead of regeneration. Culture instead of conversion. The natural in all things, the supernatural in nothing."

And, as Dr. Strong, of Rochester Theological Seminary, writes: "We seem to be on the verge of another Unitarian defection. We need a new vision of the Saviour to convince us that Jesus is lifted above space and time, that His existence antedated creation, that He conducted the march of Hebrew history, that He was born of a virgin, suffered on the cross, rose from the dead, and now lives forever more, the Lord of the universe, the

---

* "Life of Jesus," p. 264.

only God with whom we have to do, our Saviour here and our Judge hereafter."

PRIMITIVE AGES AND THE SUPERNATURAL.

As the supernatural is of necessity exceptional, and must only occur at marked historical periods, especially at those creative epochs, when some great Providential beginning is made, it is just to regard it with the utmost caution. We see how large a sphere it has wielded in the world's childhood and how strong a hold it has upon the ignorant, and that irrational and hideous superstitions have often been its progeny. But abuses and excesses do not invalidate a principle. There is great force in the fact that in uncultured peoples, the simplicities and germinal truths manifest themselves with greatest power. Intuitive truths and innate beliefs are weakened by those complexities and elaborations of thought and life which weigh down the spirit's freedom and originality, and obscure great cardinal, elemental ideas.

It is not, therefore, against, but makes for their verity, that belief in the invisible, in prayer, Providence, the miracle and divine intervention, have been so pronounced in what are called the child-ages of the world. Confronting the same dread mysteries of sin and pain and death as we, yet their minds not materialized by scientific drill, and their faith not weakened by disproportioned culture of reason, it was inevitable that early peoples should walk more "as seeing the invisible," and have a firmer grasp upon the great supersensible verities of the universe.

Whatever evolution teaches, and however much it has narrowed the range of the supernatural, by tracing results to heretofore unseen and unimagined second causes, it has not at all disproved the supernatural. "To attribute the potency we find in evolution to chemical and physical forces, as does Haeckel," writes Walker, in "Christian Theism and a Spiritual Monism," "instead of to some supernatural agency, does not lessen the mystery one whit, nor make it the less a divine work; it only throws us back upon the play of those wider, law-ordered forces which constitute the universe, through which the divine reason acts." *

But, argues Professor Foster in the "Finality of the Christian Religion," in the course of an argument against the credibility of miracles: "We may

* Part I., chap. ix., 173.

not suppose that there is a twofold activity in God, a natural and a supernatural. Rather, natural law itself is the will of God; in which case it is impossible to see how God, beside this will of His, could have another will, how anything could happen which did not happen according to law. But belief in the miraculous logically implies that the natural and historical order is not so constituted that all of the divine ends admit of being attained thereby. God finds resistance to be overcome in His own moral order. As Höffding says, it is as though there were two Gods, the one operative in the customary course of things, the other correcting in single instances the work of the first."

But why may we not suppose "a twofold activity in God"? Who has limited the Infinite to one kind of action? Why should His energy and wisdom be alone shown in creative activity, and not equally in administering that which He has created? That God should lock Himself up in the creation the moment He had made it, that He must forever be hidden and helpless behind the laws of nature, and that He could never draw near in extraordinary glory and power, would make of this universe a piece of cold, hard, pitiless mechanism.

And this is Professor Foster's conclusion with respect to that divine intervention which brought such glad, glorious tidings to our sin-smitten, death-ridden earth—the Incarnation. Of it he says: "Christ was not the incarnate Son of God, but only a man of clear religious intuition. He shared the errors of His age, and the idea of His absolute sinlessness is no result of historical study."

How much more rational and logical is the conclusion of Christendom, when, from a study of all the momentous phenomena, it pronounces the verdict voiced by the concurrence of two thousand years: a supernatural Person, Christ came in a supernatural way, with supernatural powers, to do a supernatural work.

SCIENTISTS AND THE SUPERNATURAL.

As philosophical thought strengthens our belief in the transcendence as well as in the immanence of God,—in the fact that He is not only in His works by an all and ever-permeating presence, but also over them by a free personal will,—so neither does science antagonize this truth. Haeckel, the great exponent of anti-supernaturalism, is compelled to make this admission of the change produced in leading scientists, by their gathering larger premises of scientific fact and by ripening maturity of reflection. He says: "This entire change of philosophical principles, which we find in Wundt, as we found it in Kant, Virchow, DuBois, Reymond, Baer, Romanes and others, is very interesting. In their youth these able and talented scientists embraced the whole field of biological research in a broad survey and made strenuous efforts to find a unifying, natural (monistic) basis for their knowledge. In their later years they concluded that this was not attainable and entirely abandoned the idea," * and reversed their opinions, embracing belief in a supersensible first cause.

And with Huxley affirming that the divine miraculous intervention is intrinsically possible and wholly a question of evidence, and with such leading philosophers and scientists as Lord Kelvin, Sir Oliver Lodge and Professor Henry James affirming their belief in the supernatural, Christians have no reason to be shaken in their faith. Even that liberal but incisive thinker, Amiel, cannot solve the mysteries of time and history without essential admission of the supernatural. He writes in his

* "Riddle of the Universe," p. 102.

"Journal Intime": "The supernatural is now the stone of stumbling. It might be possible to agree on the idea of the divine; but, no, that is not the question—the chaff must be separated from the good grain. The supernatural is miracle, and miracle is an objective phenomenon independent of all preceding causality. Now, miracle thus understood cannot be proved experimentally, and, besides, the subjective phenomena are left out of account in the definition. Men will not see that miracle is a perception of the soul, a vision of the divine behind nature, which reveals to us the heavenly powers prompting and directing human action. For the indifferent there are no miracles. It is only the religious souls who are capable of recognizing the finger of God in certain given facts." *

Even the destructive critic, Schmiedel, while resolving the New Testament miracles into a spiritual illusion somewhat after Strauss's visionary hypothesis, yet admits the possibility of miracles. He says: "It would be clearly wrong to start with any such postulate as that miracles are impossible. Such a proposition rests upon a theory of the uni-

* "Journal Intime," p. 193.

verse, not upon exhaustive examination of all the events spoken of as miracles. The present examination will not start from the proposition that miracles are impossible."

CHAPTER XVIII.

THE SUPERNATURAL FUNDAMENTAL TO RELIGION.

THE question of the supernatural is that of the hour. A ringing call is sounding through the air to face the true issue, the reality of God's supernatural interference in the history of man versus the universal reign of unmodified law. The question is not whether the old evangelical scheme needs some adjustments to adapt it to our present knowledge, but whether its most fundamental conception, the very idea of the gospel, is *true*. A religion founded upon God's self-revelation of Himself, or a pure rationalism by which truth in religion is attained as it is in physics, or any other realm of knowledge—these are the antitheses. The line of cleavage runs just here. Can the supernatural facts of Christianity be discarded and the life-giving doctrines saved? The answer is, that Christianity is not primarily a system of ethics or moral truths, but a series of divine acts moving historically from the beginning of the Old Testament interventions to the manifestation of God in the incarnation of Jesus Christ. These historical facts are of the very essence of the religion. How strongly Paul felt this when he argued, "For if Christ be not raised your faith is vain." * He does not make the fact of the resurrection a sequence on the doctrine, but he builds the doctrine upon the fact. It is because he is convinced of the supersensible fact of the resurrection, that he believes Christ to be the Lord of Life.

The vital place of the supernatural in religion was given in the significant answer of the French critic to Compte, when the positivist philosopher asked him if he thought he could establish his new religion of humanity. "Yes," was the response, "if you can be crucified for it and rise again." And Harnack and Renan assume the same integral place for it, when the former says that from the empty Easter grave went forth the creative power of the gospel, and when the latter declares that Christianity was built upon the faith of a woman —the testimony of Magdalene that she had seen the risen Lord.

The truth here cannot be better expressed than in the words of the late Rev. William R. Hun-

* 1 Cor. xv. 17.

tington, D. D., rector of Grace Church, New York City, in the "Gospel of the Infancy." "Concerning the so-called new theology, in so far as it is an attempt to eviscerate the New Testament of the miraculous element, I am persuaded that it is doomed to failure. Can a gospel of the resurrection etherealized into a ghost-story account for the upspringing of Christendom? Will preachers be helped to uplift the people, when criticism shall have dwarfed the 'holy nativity' into a common birth, and the precious death into a common dying? Will not sensible people quickly reach the conclusion that the whole story, from first to last, is but a cunningly devised fable? I feel more and more deeply that the choice lies between Christianity and no Christianity. Robert Elsemereism is not going to be the religion of the future. Its exponents are trading on borrowed capital and use only cut flowers."

The supernatural is not, then, as is often alleged, the weakness of Christianity, an impeding luggage, which, if we be wise, we will disload. It is not Christianity that upholds the miracles, but they are an arm of its strength. The apostles saw this, and, accordingly everywhere, to overcome a hostile world, preached the resurrection. They realized that the greatest supernatural fact of Christianity was also its sword of conquering power.

We find the same true of the apostolical fathers. It is the resurrection of which they bear witness. "Let us, brethren," writes Clemens Romanus, "contemplate the resurrection, the raising of Jesus Christ by the power of God from the dead." * "I greatly rejoice," writes Ignatius, "beloved, with you in our Lord Jesus Christ, whom God raised from the dead, having loosed the bands of the grave." †
Again, "Christ was truly raised. His Father quickening Him, even as after the same manner, His Father will raise us up who believe on Him." ‡

RELIGION NEEDS THE SUPERNATURAL.

The reason of the convincing force of a great supernatural work is that it brings us into immediate contact with God. In nature we see Him but as a Power, here we behold Him as a Person. The original witnesses of the miracles felt this when they cried out: "This is none other than the power of God." "This is of a truth that prophet that should come into the world." §

* First Epistle, chap. xxiv.
† Epistle to Philippians, chap. i.
‡ Epistle to Trallians, chap. ix.   § John vi. 40.

When men saw that Christ did works such as no mere man could do, they believed in the divinity of His person and mission. Just so to-day, it is the basis of Christianity in a supernatural origin that gives it its divine sanction and arms it with converting power.

Even in the missionary field, while it is so far above reason and excites inevitable opposition, yet it is in preaching it and in the convincing force of these miraculous facts that lies the missionary's only hope of success. Dr. James S. Dennis, so great an authority on missions, on account of his long observation and experience, tells us that it is these miraculous records and features that incite the profoundest interest of the listener. To put it, as Dr. Dennis says, in the language of the heathen, when he hears the supernatural facts of the gospel: "If you have news straight from God, I will hear you."

Sabatier thus is compelled to admit that "all religions have asserted a divine, supernatural intervention in their origin, and have rested their primary sanction in miracles." * J. Stuart Mill saw this necessity truly enough, and so, in his "Logic,"

* "Religions of Authority and the Spirit," p. 201.

when he maintains that all superhuman acts and influences on the mind recorded in history were but a dream, at once reaches the conclusion that all "definite faith and acts of devotion and prayer are but childish superstition."

So John Morley, in a thoughtful paper, discusses the question, "Why decay in dogmatic beliefs leads to a decline in Christian ethics," as he sees that it does. And Prof. Woodberry, in his "Makers of Literature," accounts for relapse in public and social morals by the passing of belief in the inspiration of the Bible, and the consequent de-Christianization of the modern world.

Well, then, may we say with Walker: "In this we see clearly the source of our highest inspiration, and discern that the want of a real belief in these verities, is just the deepest want of our time. When men cut themselves off from the supernatural, they sever themselves from the Fountain of spiritual power, and we need not wonder at the result."* Or, as writes a great thinker and theologian, Dr. M. Valentine, "Christian theology can never consent to obliterate the valid distinction between the natural and the supernatural self-manifestation of

* "Christian Theism and a Spiritual Monism," p. 8.

God, without giving up the special soteriological character of the latter, and permitting Christianity to drop down to the rank of a mere human product, as one among the simple nature religions of the world."

CHRISTIANITY WILL NOT YIELD THE SUPERNATURAL.

The Christian Church, then, shows a true insight when she refuses to surrender or attribute little emphasis to the supernatural. But she realizes that it is the secret of her evangelical power. Not for a moment will she abate her belief in the divinity of her Founder, or in the validity of the mighty acts of God inaugurating her origin.

All the stress of present opposition will not drive her to so suicidal a position as to surrender the holy mysteries which at once veil her truths and are their divine investiture. As writes the acute German thinker, Rothe: "Our duty nowadays is to establish the authority of the *supernatural* in Christianity in the strictest sense of the word, but with unconditional exclusion of the magical." *

St. Augustine profoundly remarks: "All things begin in some wonder, and in some wonder all

* Still Hours," p. 323

SUPERNATURAL FUNDAMENTAL TO RELIGION. 149

things end." As all scientific researches at last reach a gulf of mystery, a deep of wonder which they cannot fathom, as in the origin of life and personality, so was the new Christian life introduced into our world by a mysterious and wonderful series of supernatural acts. And it is in the fact that, whenever men go back to these birthdays of Christianity, they come face to face with God, wherein lies her unique authority. And if men are to accept her as a safe and trustworthy guide for their souls to the haven of eternal life, ever must she, as in all the ages of the past, affirm her supernatural credentials, and especially that miracle of miracles, the Resurrection of her Founder from the dead.

In the fine words of Forsyth : " With all her liberalism, the Church must be positive. She must insist on the autonomy of faith in the matter of knowledge and certainty. She must descend on the world out of heaven from God. Her note is the *supernatural* note which distinguishes incarnation from immanence, redemption from evolution, the kingdom of God from mere spiritual progress, and the Holy Spirit from mere spiritual process." *

* " Positive Preaching and Modern Mind," p. 121.

THE "NATURE" RELIGIONS AND THEIR FAILURE.

Ex-President Eliot has lately thus expressed the idea that a "New Religion," destitute of the supernatural, is soon to supplant Christianity: "The New Religion will not be based on authority or bound by dogma or creed. There will be no supernatural element; it will place no reliance upon anything but the laws of nature. It will admit no sacraments except natural, hallowed customs, and it will deal with natural interpretations of such rites."

In view of the wide publicity of such statements and the tendency of many to take them seriously, it is pertinent to this discussion to summon in review the various Nature Religions. That is, let us glance at the great world religions evolved from the natural reason and compare or contrast them with that supernatural one—Christianity—which has not come up from man, but down from God.

Buddhism, the religion having, perhaps, the largest number of adherents in the world, denies creation and ignores any Ruler or Governor of the world. It repudiates immortality and progress, the highest development of the soul leading to Nirvana, or annihilation.

Brahmanism is a system of pantheism, in which God is resolved into such a spiritual haze that His personality is lost, and nature, the soul, time, space and matter become "illusions." Says the "Vedanta": "From the highest state of Brahma to the lowest condition of a straw all things are delusion."

Confucianism is, in fact, no religion; has no real conception of a Deity or of responsibility to a Supreme Ruler, is but a utilitarian scheme, and, accordingly, lacks any motive and sanction, even, for morality.

In the religions of *Zoroaster*, *Egypt* and the *Eddas*, dual gods, light and darkness, Ormazd and Ahriman, Osiris and Typhon, Odin and Loki, in eternal battle, leave the universe in a hopeless dualism between the forces of good and evil.

Mohammedanism is, indeed, monotheistic, but it represents God as pure will, absolute power, without compassion or love, and demands the submission of slaves instead of the loving obedience of children. Hence, it has no sense of universality or brotherhood, and uses the sword as its only means of propagation. Its sensual and selfish heaven makes impossible all pure and noble ideals.

In the *Greek* and *Roman* pantheon, polytheism carried variety to the extreme of disorder. The Deities are, at first, identified with, then raised to, personifications of Nature. They are anthropomorphic to the furthest degree, often exhibiting the lowest passions, and resorting to the meanest and most cowardly artifices. They are not supreme, but subject to a mysterious and inexorable fate, and, utterly lacking holiness, they could exert little or no authority or moral influence over the actions of men.

Such are those Nature Religions—"Religions growing wild," as Martensen aptly terms them—which the powers of man's natural reason have been able to summon from the vasty deep of the unknown. And it is to these vague guesses, to these blind gropings after truth, to these misty, confused, irreconcilable hypotheses utterly impotent to give any certain answer to the mind, any sure comfort to the heart, or any compelling motive to the will, that ex-President Eliot and those of his school would lead us as the supreme achievement of modern progress.

And are we to believe that the world is ready to set up these impotent theories for that religion, founded upon the supernatural Person, direct communion with the Father, and absolute authority of Him who was the Truth itself, which has upset kingdoms, reversed the currents of the ages, swept the civilized world, transformed barbarous cruelty into brotherhood and sweet charity, and set mankind forward on its course with a new inspiration of courage and eternal hope? Scarcely.

"The tree is known by its fruits."

Where the Nature Religions have wretchedly and despairingly failed, the religion of revelation, of pure monotheism, of a God immanent in nature and man, yet not losing His transcendence and personality, of a righteous Deity who is yet a Father, of reconciliation of the dualism between good and evil, of atonement for sin, of faith in divine companionship and consolation, of triumph over death, and of a sure pledge of eternal life, has mightily and gloriously succeeded.

And not until this earth turns backward on its axis will this modern age yield up this, its most precious heritage, for chaff and dust and ashes.

CHAPTER XIX.

PROTESTANTISM VERSUS ROMANISM.

The Roman Catholic Church bases its claim to be an authoritative representation of Christianity largely upon antiquity. It has perpetuated the faith of old. It has held it through an unbroken chain of witnesses. As Christianity is an historical religion, this claim, if true, is just. The faith preached by the Founder, and the usages traceable to apostolic practice, give the most authentic expression to the religion. And the greater the antiquity of these, the closer their contact with the original sources, the more apt are they to be truly Christian. The stream may be greatly corrupted as it flows afar, but as we approach the fountain, we find it in its original purity.

And it is just this test which exposes the groundlessness of many distinctly Romish claims. Not alone in lesser features, but in those great outlines which differentiate Romanism from Protestantism, and which are vital to the former's claim to be the only true Church of Christ, we find its claims to the authority of history unsubstantiated by this period.

The whole external fabric of the Roman Church, reared upon the premise that an ecclesiastical order was instituted by the apostles, and that such order was essential to a truly constituted Church, is invalidated by this testimony, for, not alone are many of the foremost fathers utterly ignorant of such a polity, but even those who are acquainted with it do not deem it of apostolical origin, or to have been perpetuated by succession. The thesis upon which the churches of Protestantism stand, that their various forms of government are secondary and matters of freedom, is the one we here find in force.

THE PATRISTIC PERIOD PROTESTANT.

The assertion that Peter was the first bishop of Rome, and that the bishop of Rome was invested with a primacy over the other great episcopal sees, has not left a single trace in the records of this period. Paul is referred to more frequently, and in far more glowing terms, as the real founder, after Christ, of the Church. There is no reference to Peter ever having occupied the see of Rome, a thing inconceivable if it had been the fact.

The Lord's Supper is not treated as "a sacrifice, presenting anew, in an unbloody form, the bloody offering of the cross." * There is not the least hint to suggest that it should be given only in one kind to the laity, while the priests partook of both kinds. The fiction that the body includes the blood, and and that therefore the cup is unnecessary, has not as yet been formulated in a brain wiser than that of the Master Himself, who when He said, "Drink ye all of it," gave no intimation of such a limited use.

On the contrary, the instruction given in the Didache, or Teaching of the Twelve Apostles, viz., "Let no one eat or *drink* of the Eucharist," etc., † and the prayer before the Lord's Supper in the Constitutions of the Holy Apostles: "Do thou show this bread to be the body of thy Christ, and the *cup* to be the blood of thy Christ, that those who are partakers thereof may obtain the remission of their sins, and be strengthened for piety," ‡ prove conclusively that the wine as well as the bread was distributed to the whole congregation.

There is no Mariolatry. Mary is never called "the mother of God." She is never spoken of as a Mediator, through whose motherly heart the com-

* Roman Catechism. † Chaps. ix. and x. ‡ Book VIII., chap. xii.

passion of her blessed Son will be the more readily reached. There are no stronger expressions respecting her than the Scripture ones, or than any Protestant would justly use. Again and again is she referred to, but with no suggestion of more than a becoming extraordinary regard. " The Word was truly born of the virgin." " Christ made for Himself a body of the seed of the virgin." " The virginity of Mary was hidden from the prince of this world " —such and no more, is the honor accorded her.

THE FICTION OF INDULGENCES.

We discover nothing of such a doctrine as that " Indulgences remit the temporal punishment due to sin by applying to us the superabundant satisfaction of the blessed Virgin Mary and of the saints, which merits and satisfactions are the spiritual treasury of the Church." * It is not, as Tetzel said, the clink of the coin in the Church treasury for the indulgence that sets free the soul from purgatory, but heart repentance for sin. As writes Hermas: " He who has sinned must repent with his whole heart and be exceedingly humble and contrite, and then God will assuredly have compassion when He

* Roman Catholic Catechism of Christian Doctrine—Plenary Council of Baltimore.

sees the heart of the penitent pure from every evil thing." * Luther, when he nailed up his ninety-five theses against indulgences on the door of the Castle Church at Wittenberg—"the blows of his hammer," as Carlyle says, "echoing round the world"—gave no more evangelical definition than this of repentance.

Nor do the apostolic fathers lay any claim to supernatural powers in the Roman manner. There are no visions and healings by the Virgin Mary. There is not even reference to the anointing with oil in sickness, which would imply that the words of St. James were of but temporary application.

There is no sacrament of extreme unction, or it would certainly have been used in the instances of the last hours of holy martyrs recorded.

The gift of tongues is not perpetuated.

There are no records of healings by the great spiritual leaders of the period, about whom legendary honors would naturally have accrued. Nor were miraculous powers ascribed to the relics of the martyrs. If such would have been the case with anyone it would have been with Ignatius, held in such extraordinary veneration during his

* Pastor, Book III., "Similitude," viii.

life. Yet it is stated that his holy remains were conveyed to Antioch and deposited in the church for honorable memory alone.

Fasting was lightly practiced, but there was no asceticism. There was no celibacy of the clergy. There was no purgatory. There was no monasticism. There was no asking the prayers of the dead.

In short, the review of the whole field of belief and practice brings us into the atmosphere of Protestantism. The distinguishing traits of Romanism belong to a later period. If it be contended that many of these have been originated by the Church herself exercising a legitimate right, there must not then, however, be assumed for them that great authority which justly belongs to antiquity. That a doctrine was originated at a later period, as for example, purgatory by Cyprian,* but was entirely unknown at an earlier date, severs it altogether from Christian antiquity, from any sanction of apostolic or divine origin whatever.

NO PAPACY IN THE EARLY CHURCH.

We discover in this era, moreover, not a germ of the dogma of papal infallibility. How could there

* Epistle, lv. 20.

be such when no one had heard of a Pope? And, especially, there have arisen no signs of that doctrine of the supremacy of the Church over the State, which was yet to darken all Christendom with its huge dimensions, and to hold mankind in the dungeon of spiritual slavery. This tyrannical dogma our age has outlived by the achievement of that religious toleration, which Canon Liddon calls the finest fruit of the last four centuries. And yet the Pope, in our very day, has re-asserted it, affirming in the "Papal Syllabus": "The Church has the right of applying force and the temporal power of the Episcopacy is not the gift of the State and may not be recalled by the State."

To any historical authority for this tremendous claim, with all its grave possibilities, Canon Mozley truly replies: "The very earliest Christianity, that which is co-eval with the fountain-head, is the most modern in its tone in this respect. The Church is a spiritual society to educate us by revealed doctrine for an eternal existence; the State is a temporal society to preserve order and peace and to maintain human life under the proper visible conditions. The whole weight of facts, the whole weight of truth, is irresistibly against the Roman

PROTESTANTISM VERSUS ROMANISM. 161

claim. This is a point on which Christianity and civilization, which look suspiciously at each other at times, entirely join hands; they speak one language; they abjure with one mouth, force, as the property of the Church, and force as applicable to religion at all. The earth must roll back on its axis again before the moral sense of society recants on this question." *

ROMANISM'S FALSE ANTIQUITY.

One of the strongest arrows in the quiver of Romanism is her boasted antiquity. But the study of the sub-apostolic age brings out beyond dispute the fact that true antiquity pertains to Protestantism, that its doctrines have the sanction of that primitive antiquity which outweighs a thousand to one the authority of later, degenerated ages.

This feature Luther took acute advantage of in his struggle with Rome. He was too little of a radical and iconoclast to hope for success in the conflict with so formidable and venerable a hierarchy without the support of any authority. Herein lay his signal divergence from Savonarola, and the

* University Sermons, "The Roman Council," p. 21.

secret of the latter's failure. So Luther appealed not alone to the Scriptures, but to the sub-apostolic era, in which the gospel teachings and the traditions of the Church yet remained pure. And, supported by this legitimate and powerful authority, he won the confidence of Christendom and prevailed.

Rome can make no valid claim to authority. Eck admitted that the Protestants had the Scriptures, but claimed the fathers. But history shows that the Christian Church, in its pure apostolic phase, gives no countenance to Romish traditions. The argument from an era of such vast authoritative significance is conclusively with Protestantism.

CHAPTER XX.

THE PRIMITIVE CHURCH AND CHARITY.

OF the new moral ideals taught by Jesus to men, none stood in more pointed contrast to the standards of the ancient world than that of charity. The Jew, indeed, had been taught the duty of brotherhood, but that he understood as narrowed to his own race.

Pagan life was characterized by the severest form of selfishness. Unbounded luxury and extravagance went side by side with extreme poverty and hopeless misery. Nowhere in history have social contrasts been so startling as in this period. Some reveled in the extremest excesses of opulence, while others were submerged in the lowest squalor, misery and vice.

"In Imperial Rome a whole population might be trembling lest they should be starved by the delay of an Alexandrian corn-ship, while the upper classes were squandering a fortune at a single banquet, drinking out of myrrhine and jeweled vases worth hundreds of pounds, and feasting on the brains of peacocks and the tongues of nightingales. Vitellius set on the table at one banquet two thousand fishes and seven thousand birds, and in less than eight months spent on feasts a sum that would now amount to several millions." *

As poverty is the shadow cast by inordinate wealth, so the accumulation of such enormous fortunes and such recklessly lavish expenditure could only subsist with a corresponding depth of poverty and wretchedness. This seems to have caused no concern among the political rulers, and, on the part of the citizens, there was no evidence of commiseration to relieve it. No societies were formed, no institutions built, and no money appropriated for relief. The burden of children was relieved by infanticide, and the sick, the suffering and the incurable were left to a hopeless fate.

INHUMANITY OF THE PAGAN WORLD.

"In reading the works of Cicero or Seneca, one must glean and glean for single humanitarian sentiments. Their writings are exquisite in form, and polished like statues, but they are without heart or

* "Early Days of Christianity," Farrar, p. 2.

humanity. To-day all literature is working for the once despised and unbefriended classes."*

Christ, by the parable of the Good Samaritan, taught that we owed a duty of pity and relief to the unfortunate. And in that remarkable phrase, which has been the inspiration of so many a charitable soul and cause: "Inasmuch as ye have done it unto one of the least of these my brethren, ye have done it unto me," † He called attention to the image of God stamped on every man, and to the Christ even in the poorest and most unfortunate.

Not till Christianity appeared did the love of one's neighbor, in the true sense of the word, exist. Christianity introduced humanity into the world and inculcated the virtue of compassion. Care for the sick and poor, which has played so famous a part in the history of the Christian world, was one of its happy fruits. That spirit of love, of resignation, of self-sacrifice, which is the loveliest and noblest part of the moral life, proceeded from Christianity, from the cross of Christ.‡

---

* "Great Books as Life Teachers," Newell Dwight Hillis, p. 75.
† Matt. xxv. 40.
‡ Luthardt's "Fundamental Truths of Christianity," Lecture X.

Accordingly, the idea and duty of charity were impressed upon the early disciples. And so vital a part of Christianity was this deemed that, at the very outset of the Church's history, we find in Acts vi. that regular provision was made for a daily ministration of supplies for the needs of the poor. This duty was considered only secondary to that of its ministry of the word, and was at first discharged by the apostles themselves, but asserting that "it is not reason that we should leave the word of God and serve tables,"* deacons from among the laymen were selected to be "appointed over this business."

CHRISTIAN DEACONS AND DEACONESSES.

The diaconate thus was originally instituted as a ministry of mercy. Although its powers were subsequently enlarged, yet its primary purpose was the oversight and administration of this work of practical beneficence, which ever grew larger and greater with the increasing spread of the Church. "The deacons," says Dean Stanley, "became the first preachers of Christianity; they were the first evangelists, because they were the first to find their way to the homes of the poor.

* Acts vi. 2.

THE PRIMITIVE CHURCH AND CHARITY. 167

They were the constructors of the most solid and durable of the institutions of Christianity, viz., the institutions of charity and beneficence." *

A female diaconate likewise was instituted for the same work of relief, especially among those of their own sex. According to the Apostolical Constitutions, faithful and holy women were to be ordained as deaconesses, because the Church had use for them in many necessities. They were to minister to women in sickness and distress, relieve the saints in prison, and, in general, to engage in such works of charity and relief as heathen opinion would not allow male deacons to perform.

Accordingly, the Didache, or Teaching of the Twelve Apostles, gives instructions for the duties of deacons who are to have charge of " the distribution of alms as prescribed in the gospel of our Lord.† Polycarp also charges that this ministry of mercy should not be overlooked by the pastoral office itself, but that " ministers should be compassionate and merciful to all, bringing back those that wander, visiting all the sick, and not neglecting the widow, the orphan, or the poor." ‡ Again:

* " Early Days of Christianity," p. 171.
† Chap. xv.   ‡ Epistle, chap. vi.

"When you can do good, defer it not, because alms deliver from death." * Clement urges the same virtue, thus : " He who takes upon himself the burden of his neighbor ; he who, in whatsoever he abounds, helps another who is deficient ; he who, whatsoever things he has received from God, by distributing these to the needy, is an imitator of Christ." † Ignatius : " Let not widows be neglected. Be thou after the Lord, their protector." ‡

THE IMITATION OF CHRIST.

These exhortations abound on the pages of this primitive literature. The conception of Christian piety was that of the imitation of Christ, "who pleased not Himself," and that of the maxim of Paul : "Look not every man on his own things, but every man also on the things of others." § The poor, the orphans and the widows were regarded as the precious " treasures of the Church," and to sacrifice for them was esteemed both a privilege and a joy.

Nothing, indeed, is more impressive than the sight of these early Christians, stigmatized by the society of the times, persecuted by the civil power,

---

* Epistle, chap. x. † Epistle to Diognetus, chap. x.
‡ Epistle to Polycarp, chap. iv. § Phil. ii. 4.

impoverished and suffering all manner of hardship themselves, yet, instead of growing hardened and embittered, overflowing with kindliness and sympathy for the suffering, whether of the Church or of the Pagans, and out of their own dire needs and extremity making large and regular contributions to human relief. Even Gibbon is compelled to admit this fine exercise of generosity. He says: " The uses to which their liberality was applied reflected honor on the religious society. The sacred patrimony for the poor was distributed to support widows and orphans, the lame, the sick and the aged of the community, to comfort strangers and pilgrims, and to alleviate the misfortunes of strangers and captives. A generous intercourse of charity united the most distant provinces, and the smaller congregations were cheerfully assisted by the alms of their more opulent brethren. Such an institution, which paid less regard to the merit than to the distress of the object, very materially conduced to the progress of Christianity. The Pagans, who were actuated by a sense of humanity, while they derided the doctrines, acknowledged the benevolence of the new sect." *

* " Decline and Fall of the Roman Empire," Vol. I., chap. xv

From this review it is manifest that, while the first aim of the primitive Church was to preach to the soul the necessity of religion, spirituality, the forgiveness of sins, and inward regeneration, so far was it from neglecting the needs of the body, that, hand in hand with its spiritual, went its charitable work.

And from the principles and practices of this age have sprung all those benevolences, from the merciful orders of the middle ages to the sisters of charity in the Roman Catholic Church, and the Protestant Deaconesses, numbering their thousands, and the institutions of mercy and relief which now overspread the globe.

When it is charged by unbelieving critics that the modern Church has lost the spirit of the early Church in this respect, the conclusive answer is given by the facts. The activity in works of mercy and relief by the churches of the civilized and heathen world is unparalleled, or, at least, unsurpassed by any preceding age. All the mighty streams of charity either issue directly from the Christian Church, or have arisen from the influence of her teachings and standards.

Prof. Shailer Matthews thus forcibly states this

point: " Until there can be shown some other social institution or movement which can boast an equal record of social reforms—of slavery ended, of life protected, of woman ennobled, of children educated, of homes sanctified, of schools and missions and martyrs—your social reformer had best give himself a course in church history." *

The real edge of this modern criticism of the Church with respect to charity is disbelief in her as an institution of religion. Men of the world do not believe in her faith, in the divinity of her Founder, and in the power of the gospel. Hence, they would like to see her abandon her prophetical office towards the souls of men, and devote herself wholly to philanthropical work. But the position of the Church is that she owes her life to her faith, that philanthropy is the child of religion, that the gospel she proclaims must first change and renew the hearts of men before they will burn with the sense of brotherhood. She holds, with Carlyle: " Show me what a man or nation believes, and I will tell you the character and the deeds of that person or people."

The Church understands the secret of her power

* " The Church and the Changing Order," p. 168.

too well, and too thoroughly understands the purpose of her critics to cut off her right arm by abandoning religion and faith and the cure of souls for the work of charity. She will keep the fountain strong and pure under the throne and altar of God, knowing that thence will flow the mightiest streams of beneficence. And she will ever remember that the soul of charity is charity to the soul.

CHAPTER XXI.

THE CHURCH AND SOCIAL REFORM.

CLOSELY connected with the theme of the preceding chapter is the relation of the Church to social, economic, civic and governmental efforts for the amelioration of bad conditions and for the uplift and well-being of the masses. That Christianity concerns itself, first of all, with the soul and with the spiritual side is no reason why it should not seek the good of the whole man and his betterment in all the spheres and relations of life. This it does primarily in that the greater includes the less, and it does it indirectly in that when men's ideals are changed or when right principles are inculcated, the leaven tends to spread through all the series of social strata until the whole is leavened.

There remains the question, however, in how far it is correct, judicious and safe for the Church, as an organization, directly to ally itself with distinctively ethical, humanitarian and reformatory movements as such. Social reformers are insistent that the Church should take direct part in these propaganda, that the pulpit should make them its theme, and that all the forces of the Christian organization should be thrown into the arena. The contention is that the Church is losing a large opportunity for usefulness, and also declining in influence with the masses, whereas a contrary policy would win over to her great numbers who now remain aloof, and vastly accelerate her own growth.

The demand is also made that in the curriculum of our theological seminaries less time be given to such studies as Biblical Exegesis, Church History, Systematic Theology, etc., and that a larger sphere be allotted to the practical concerns of every-day living. We should have more chairs for the investigation of topics suggested by Modern Sociology, and the studies of students should more profitably be directed along sociological lines. It is charged that our theological seminaries are doing little, if anything, to equip ministers for the task of reaching the man with the dinner pail, of bridging over the chasm between the Church and labor.

The question is a vital one, and, as bearing on the legitimate scope of the Church's agency, and also on the favorable or unfavorable estimate held of her by the public at large, should be carefully considered and wisely and decisively answered by every conscientious minister.

THE CHURCH AND SOCIOLOGY.

The manner in which our Lord met these questions, as far as they confronted Him, is, for the student of practical Christianity, of the first importance. Having not Himself whereon to lay His head, and traversing on foot the fields and thoroughfares where He encountered the toiling masses, with His quick and sensitive sympathy He bore all their burdens upon His heart. No burden is more oppressive than that of political bondage. "No yoke," says Macaulay, "is so galling as that of the foreigner." Christ found His countrymen suffering under this well-nigh intolerable yoke, and a great revulsion in the popular feeling toward Him ensued when He declined to interfere.

All that He was willing to do in the premises was to lay down the cardinal guiding principle, " Render unto Cæsar the things that are Cæsar's, and unto God the things that are God's." * One of the most fruitful causes of wrong in human society is the maladministration of justice. One such aggrieved

* Mark xii. 17.

party came to our Lord as the imagined adjudicator of all rights, with a request that He intervene. But His only response was, "Man, who made me a judge or a divider over you?"* Yet, who has done so much to subvert the yoke of the oppressor, and to vindicate to nations the right of self-government, and who has so advanced the equal-handed administration of justice between strong and weak, rich and poor, as has the great Teacher?

It was not that He did not smart under the sense of pain for social wrongs and injustices, but that He felt that by embroiling Himself in battle with them He was drawn apart from the supreme mission for which He came, as a spiritual Prophet, to bear witness to the Truth, and that thereby this wider and greater sway over the well-being of mankind would be weakened. And history has vindicated His far-seeing wisdom and His well-poised judgment.

Thus says Luthardt: "Christianity introduced the era of humanity—of the rights of man. It made no changes in the external arrangements of society; it left laws and privileges, manners and conditions, customs and ranks as it found them;

* Luke xii. 14.

THE CHURCH AND SOCIAL REFORM. 177

but it introduced a new spirit into all these relations of life. It did not even externally abolish slavery; but it taught all to recognize in the slave a man, a Christian brother, and thus gave an internal blow to this objectionable institution. It raised the condition of women from a degraded to a most honorable and influential one. It made love, —which, as Montesquieu said, at the time of its introduction, still bore only a form which cannot be named,—the noblest and tenderest power of mental and spiritual life. It withdrew children, whom the heathen world had felt no scruple at destroying either before or after their birth, from the arbitrary power of their parents as mere property, and placed them under the Saviour's protection by declaring them to be by baptism children of God, and inheritors of the kingdom of heaven." *

RELIGION THE CHURCH'S AGENCY OF REFORM.

The same lesson is taught the Church by a study of the course pursued by our holy fathers. The social situation confronting them was desperate. The masses were regarded as without souls. Three-fourths of human beings were slaves, with their lives

* " Fundamental Truths of Christianity," Lecture X.

at the caprice of their masters. There was no regard for human life. Augustus sacrificed the lives of three thousand men in a sea-fight to delight the blunted moral sense of the citizens. Vices that hide from modern view, unblushingly looked out from the decorations and statuary of the palaces and public baths, as revealed in the unearthed cities of Heculaneum and Pompeii. It was almost time, one feels like saying, that such repulsive horrors should be covered by the terrible agency of the volcano. The "social evil" was universal. Plato advocated a community of wives. So deplorable was the prevalent immorality that even the Roman moralist, Seneca, wrote: "Everything is full of vices and crimes. There is a great struggle who shall exceed in turpitude. Day by day the love of sin increases and shame diminishes." * And the satirist, Juvenal, exclaims: "Truly the present is a ninth age of the world, far worse than the iron age, and one to express whose badness nature herself can furnish no name, and has produced no metal." †

And what, now, were the means taken by the

* Luthardt's "Moral Truths of Christianity," p. 345.
† Ibid.

apostolic fathers and spiritual leaders of this age to redress these shocking evils and to save society from this awful abyss of sin, vice and misery? They simply held up Christ. They preached the gospel. They called men to repentance and faith. They urged all to become believers. They insisted on Baptism and the Lord's Supper. They declared that regeneration, through the means of grace, was the only hope of the regeneration of society. They held to the power of their message to cure these vile conditions and to pour the streams of a cleansing, purifying life through all the bogs and quagmires of moral corruption.

In short, their practice reveals their conviction that religion, mediated by the Church, was society's only hope. And the more desperate the social conditions, the more definitely and positively they held the Church to her supreme function. And it is not to be doubted that in this course they were guided by a wisdom not their own. They were led by the Holy Ghost.

That a reaction from the modern tendency to make the Church chiefly a social reform bureau is beginning to appear, is shown by these recent words from the eminent thinker at the head of

Princeton University, President Woodrow Wilson:

"I believe that we have erroneously conceived the sphere of the Christian Church in our age. If my observation does not mislead me, the Christian Church nowadays is tempted to be regarded as chiefly a philanthropic institution, chiefly an instrument that shall supply the spiritual impulse which is necessary for carrying on those great enterprises which relieve the distress, distress of body and distress of mind, which so disturbs the world and so excites our pity, among those men particularly who have not had the advantages of fortune or of economic opportunity. And yet I believe that this is only a very small part of the business of the Church. The business of the Church is not to pity men. No man who has recovered the integrity of his soul is any longer the object of pity, and it is to enable him to recover that lost integrity that the Christian Church is organized."

What the minister has to do is to reveal God to men, reveal God to them in their own spirits, reveal God to them in thought and in action, re-establish the spiritual kingdom among us, by proclaiming in season and out of season that there is no explanation for anything that is not first or last a spiritual explanation, and that man cannot live by bread alone.

And this conservative, far-seeing sagacity, this strength with patience, this faith in her spiritual weapons, has characterized the Church of Christ in every age.

The first mission of the Church is spiritual. Her work is to reconstruct the moral nature. She is to awaken the soul from its death in trespasses and sins. She is to be the interpreter of Religion. She is to point men to the higher life. She is to preach to them the Word of God. She is to recreate them by the power of the Holy Ghost. She is to build them up in the image of Jesus Christ. Whatever may be her secondary activity, this spiritual and religious mission must ever be her supreme aim.

THE GOSPEL THE CHIEF AGENCY OF REFORM.

Social reform needs reinforcement just at this point. It is not enough to clean up the slums, to build school-houses with play-grounds, to appoint boards of arbitration. All these and countless other reforms are necessary and invaluable. But if they ignore God, what promise is there in them of a

completed social evolution? In addition to reform men need to feel that there is something more powerful making for social peace than even better men in a new environment. That something is God. "To make a Church a religious mixture of civil service reform, debating societies, gymnasiums, suppers, concerts, stereopticon lectures, good advice, refined negro minstrel shows and dramatic entertainments, is to bring it into competition with the variety theatre. And when the masses have to choose between that sort of church and its rival, if they have any sense left within their perplexed heads, they will choose the society theatre. That, at least, is performing its proper social function." *
The "up-to-date" minister prides himself in having his hands in everything. Paul said: "This one thing I do." He was all-absorbed in his "high calling in Christ Jesus." Such a minister gains in dignity and spiritual power far more than he loses by "leaving the Word of God to serve tables" with every propaganda labeled Social Reform. The Church must educate its members in the principles governing social conduct by bringing their lives

* "The Church and the Changing Order," Prof. Shailer Matthews, p. 158.

into vital relationship with God, and then it must leave them to act freely on political or social questions as their judgment may dictate.

And while she has had to bear many reproaches for it, and has lost much superficial applause, there is no doubt that she has thereby achieved incalculably vaster results for the well-being and progress of the race. One by one she has seen the various forms of social injustice weaken and disappear, until, under the influence of her teaching and communion, the worst evils that have darkened the course of human history are now relegated to a forgotten past, or exist but as a byword and memorial of warning.

For example, the Church as a whole in America was indignantly held to answer because it would not join many of the New England churches in an open campaign against slavery. But the Church felt that, inasmuch as slavery had a quasi-recognition in the Constitution and was held by a large body of citizens to be a political question, it was so involved with existing policies and social conditions that it was beyond its sphere directly to attack it. It assumed that the least harmful and the most thorough method to overthrow what was an undoubted evil was by turning upon it the light of gospel liberty, and asserting those generic Biblical teachings of human brotherhood, under the force of which it must inevitably disappear. And we think the dispassionate judgment of history approves the Church's long-suffering wisdom in that acute crisis.

In these lessons of history the Church can find her guiding principles for the present age with respect to the various phases of Social Reform. Take, for example, the relation of the organized Church to organized labor. Here is a statement of labor's demands by a leading representative: "The wage workers, seeing no interest, or but little interest, manifested in the Church in the human side of a religious question, or in the question of bread and butter and a decent living, have naturally drifted away from the Church to a great extent; and I am constrained to believe that they are not going back in large numbers until the Church will emphasize just as strongly the human side of the religion of Jesus Christ as it does the spiritual side."

Were the Church to yield to such an insistence, she would have to reconstruct her organization fundamentally. And such a revolutionary policy would, in the end, overthrow that power which, exerted in accord with her primary character, has been the means of removing so many a yoke from the neck of labor, and elevating the laboring classes to a position of dignity and comparative equality of opportunity such as they had never known but for her potent, beneficial influence.

THE CHURCH PRIMARILY A SPIRITUAL TEACHER.

And so, when we are told that we must make the Christian religion less divine and more human, less spiritual and more social, rather an elaborate organization for social service than a kingdom of God, simply "a union of those who love for the service of those who suffer," and disencumber the church of word and sacrament, of creed and confession, of faith and worship, of the agency and power of the Holy Spirit, and of calling men first of all " not to live by bread alone, but by every word that proceedeth out of the mouth of God," let us be on our guard.

When Christianity surrenders these, her Samson locks, at the behest of superficial social reformers, she will be false to her high and unique calling as the spiritual teacher of mankind, and she will be shorn of her reformatory power. The Church, as the visible organization of the kingdom of God—the communion of saints—can only do her ordained work in her own way, and by fidelity to her historic conservatism.

As an illustration of the effectiveness of this method, of the Church not entangling herself with compromising alliances with secularistic, social and ethical reform movements, or resorts to legal authority, Kurtz, in his "Church History," has this significant note: "The three inveterate moral plagues of the ancient world, contempt of foreign nationalities, degradation of women, and slavery, were overcome, according to Gal. iii. 28, ('For ye are all one in Christ Jesus,') by gradual elevation of inward feelings, without any violent struggle against existing laws and customs, and the consciousness of common membership in the one head in heaven, hallowed all the relationships of the earthly life." *

The Church is not a sociological lectureship. One of the chief reasons why the social influence of

* Vol. I., pp. 63, 64.

the pulpit is not greater among the masses is undoubtedly the fact, that in its zeal to get in touch with the masses it has been nagged into undertaking every sort of reform.

But, in the same proportion as the Church has been diverted from her peculiar field, has she lost not only her religious, but her general social influence. She must, therefore, in self-protection, sternly object to making religion a mere instrument for the furthering of a propaganda which is purely secular. All these efforts to induce the Church to make herself an appendage for the advancement of social reform in any of its phases is but another way of saying that she shall be secularized.

No disciple of Jesus is true to his divine Master whose heart does not thrill in response to the cries of humanity suffering from wrongs and vices. And no Church is true to its intent that is not awake to the importance of the various benevolent causes and reformatory movements, inspired by the laudable purpose to aid, help and relieve the needy and downtrodden. Ministers must not merely preach, but engage in a personal ministry of mercy. Laymen must not merely profess religion, but practice it in active lives as co-laborers in every good cause in human behalf. But all this can be most efficiently done without compromising the Church as the instrument of religion and the congregation of believers.

CHAPTER XXII.

PRIMITIVE RITES OF PUBLIC WORSHIP.

PRIMITIVE worship was naturally conducted to some extent after the pattern of the service of the synagogue and temple, as Christianity was a development on the foundation of Judaism.

The service was held in a consecrated chamber or house. The place must be holy to the Lord, set apart from common and unhallowed uses. Christianity, no less than Judaism, needed for a place of meeting with God an atmosphere permeated with religion; a sanctuary, or church, a place consecrated to prayer and praise.

CHIEF FEATURES OF THE SERVICE.

The first characteristic difference, however, was that instead of the Jewish Sabbath, public worship was observed on *Sunday*. This was because, as Justin Martyr stated in his apology to the Emperor Titus: "Sunday is the day on which we all hold our common assembly, because it is the first day on which God, having wrought a change in the dark-

ness and matter, made the world; and Jesus Christ, our Saviour, on the same day rose from the dead." *
So Ignatius writes: " Let every disciple of Christ keep the Lord's Day as a festival, the resurrection day, the queen and chief of all the days of the week." †   The Didache likewise enjoins: " Every Lord's Day do ye gather yourselves together." ‡
This was the most important symbol of the decisive break with Judaism, and the claim of Christianity to be a unique and the only true religion.

The singing of *hymns* was from the earliest time, after the example of Christ and the apostles (Matt. xxvi. 30, and Acts xvii. 25), an important feature of the service. " Spiritual Songs," as the Psalms, or paraphrases of such Scriptures as were worshipful were selected. The hymn was a veritable prayer, offered to God, and not a sensuous appeal to human emotion.

LECTIONARY OF SCRIPTURE LESSONS.

The reading of the *Scriptures* formed from the earliest date a principal and fundamental part of the worship of the Christians, as it ever had of the Jews. At first, Old Testament lessons were read,

* " First Apology," chap. lxvii.
† " Epistle to Magnesians," chap. x.   ‡ Chap. xiv.

but later, when they had been written, the selections were made from the Gospels and Epistles.

The writings of the apostolic fathers themselves, such as the Pastor of Hermas and the Epistle of Clement of Rome were also often read, but only for edification and not with the authority of the inspired writings. " These writings were very far from being thereby placed on an equality, or made co-ordinate with the canonical Scriptures, and, least of all, in the primitive times of Christianity," * which we are sketching.

At first, these lessons were taken at will from any part of the Scriptures, but later, a regular *lectionary* came to be appointed. " By the end of the second century fixed tables of lessons for the Festivals had been largely adopted." † This was done evidently for two reasons: to present a more complete synopsis of the life of Christ and the essential doctrines of Christianity, and also to secure uniformity, the Church everywhere joining in the same lessons at a common time. This plan also emphasized the chief events in the life of Christ, and naturally led to the idea of a Church Year.

* Guericke's " Christian Antiquities," p. 212.
† Ibid., p. 214.

About the end of the sixth century such a lectionary or order of lessons for all the Sundays of the Christian year had been established. It is essentially the table common to the churches to-day using an historic liturgy. When the Gospel was announced it was the custom of the congregation, out of reverence to it as the Word of God, to rise. "While the Gospel is read, let all the presbyters and deacons and all the people stand up in great silence, for it is written: 'Be silent, and hear, O Israel' (Deut. xxvii. 8). And, again: 'But do thou stand there and hear'" (Deut. v. 31).*

CENTRAL PLACE OF THE SERMON.

The reading of the Scriptures was followed by the *sermon*, which was less of an ambitious, rhetorical character, and more of an expository, practical nature. The sermon, in tribute to its importance, occupied a central position in the service. The minister, as he ascended to the pulpit, prepared himself by a moment of silent prayer, a habit that no doubt guarded him from introducing secular themes, and wandering into current sensational discussions, which might attract the crowd of superficial curiosity seekers.

* "Constitutions of the Holy Apostles," Book II., sec. 7.

The sermon was followed by the *prayer* or prayers, which were considered as an answer of the congregation for the Word proclaimed and expounded. The congregation, instructed and warmed in heart and quickened in conscience, was thought to be prepared more devoutly to offer worship. This practice of the ancient Church has been reversed in the practice of the Reformed Protestant Churches. It, however, remains the usage of the Evangelical Lutheran Church throughout the world.

The attitude in prayer was standing, in contrast to the Jewish kneeling, and in testimony of the light and joy of the worshiper's approaching to God in view of the glad tidings of grace and redemption.

The prayer, according to the Didache, was prefaced by a *confession* of sins. "In the Church thou shalt acknowledge thy transgressions, and thou shalt not come near for thy prayer with an evil conscience." * This indicates a vivid sense of sin. The Lord's Prayer was most prominently used.†

---

* "Teachings of the Twelve Apostles," chap. iv.
† Ibid., chap. viii.

The sacrament of the *Lord's Supper*, which was celebrated every Sunday, constituted the central and crowning part of the service. It was preceded by an exhortation to communicants to join earnestly in the preparatory confession of sin. "The elements in the Lord's Supper were consecrated to their sacramental purpose by a prayer of praise and thanksgiving, together with a recital of the words of institution which contained a proclamation of the death of Christ."* The wine was mingled with water, indicating that it was fermented. As the principles of the Manichean sect forbade their use of wine, they communicated only in one kind—bread. This usage was condemned by the ancient Church as heretical. It insisted on communion in both kinds, *sub utraque specie*, and required this of every member.† A prayer of intercession was then offered for the whole Church and its ministers, for kings and all in authority, for soldiers and sailors, for all Christians, for the city and its inhabitants, for those in affliction or under persecution, for all the absent members of the Church, for enemies, for those who had relapsed, and for such members of

---

* Kurtz's "Church History," sec. 17, p. 62.
† Chrysostom, Hom. XVIII.

PRIMITIVE RITES OF PUBLIC WORSHIP. 195

the congregation as had fallen asleep, but who in Christ were still alive. To these prayers the congregation answered, "Amen." All then joined in the Lord's Prayer. The communicants then came to the altar and the distribution followed. A hymn and thanksgiving followed: "Now that we have received the precious body and the precious blood of Christ, let us give thanks to Him who has thought us worthy to partake of these holy mysteries," * etc. The congregation then knelt (showing that kneeling also had its proper place) for the benediction, or prayer of blessing, and the service was over.

We observe in these primitive rites of public worship a number of instructive particulars. There remains, as yet, the purity of the Gospel, with no amalgam of later Romish errors. Spirituality, reverence and dignity characterize the liturgic usages. They constitute a distinctly religious service, every tendency of which is to incite to piety and communion with God.

By the side of the prominence given the preaching of the Word, we note also the emphasis accorded the Sacrament. It is regarded as an essen-

* " Constitutions of the Holy Apostles," Book VIII., p. 15.

tial sustenance of the Christian life. A Christian lives not alone by the Word, but by the grace communicated by the sacrament, constituted by the Word. Emphasis is thus placed upon full communion with the Church as the only true position for a genuine Christian life.

And we note the *brevity* and simplicity of the service. It is so adapted to human nature as to encourage the hearty expression of the sense of worship without depressing it by tedious and redundant forms.

PUBLIC WORSHIP RESPONSIVE.

We mark, too, that this primitive worship is *responsive*. The minister is simply the leader. He does not act as its representative for the people, but the congregation takes its own part, joins audibly in the worship, and, in its own person, makes approach to the mercy-seat. The responses not only fan the devotional flame, but give all a share. This is the true ideal—congregational worship.

We observe, moreover, that the service is a thoroughly *ordered* one. It is not left to the optional guidance of unlettered laymen, tending to scenes of disorder, nor even to the caprice of the officiating minister. But the Christian consciousness, gradually acquiring a well rounded conception of a full, judicious service, expresses itself in an order, which is authoritatively prescribed, so that the service becomes representative of the pious and intelligent judgment of the whole Church.

Such an ordered service, uniting the worship of the fathers with that of their posterity, and blending in unison, by Creed, Litany, Glorias, etc., the worship of God's people in an universal service of praise, must, of necessity, be liturgic.

Bishop Lightfoot calls attention to the prayer with which Clement closes his Epistle to the Corinthians, remarking that its careful form, clustered petitions, balanced clauses and rhythmical cadences indicate no extemporaneous production, but point to it as a *liturgical* form, elaborated by time and usage. From such evidences liturgical prayers must have originated in the earliest historic periods of Christianity.

ANTIQUITY OF LITURGIC FORMS.

In the primitive period these liturgic forms or orders were used and preserved but by oral tradition. At a somewhat later period, they began to appear in written forms. The most important of these ancient liturgies are those of St. James, or of the Church of Jerusalem; the liturgy of

St. Mark, or of the Church of Alexandria, and the Clementine Liturgy, that given in the eighth book of the Apostolical Constitutions. Although these liturgies are not the work of the apostles whose names they bear, internal evidence proves beyond dispute that they are not later than the latter part of the second century.

And, as at the time we meet them, they are elaborately constructed and of wide authority, and since such common forms must have had slow growth, it is reasonable to conclude that their historic roots strike far back into the antecedent past, and not improbably into the apostolic age. Thus, in the year 347, we find Cyril, Bishop of Jerusalem, instructing his catechumens in the prescribed church services and giving them the *rationale* of them, assuming that the order is a settled, well-known and venerable one, handed down, at least, from sub-apostolic times.

These were all true liturgies; they were adapted to the use of the congregation. The worship was responsive throughout; the people reply at all the appropriate places, "*Domine Miserere;*" "*Miserere Nostri,*" "*Deus Salvator Noster,*" etc. They repeat aloud the *oratio dominica*—the Lord's

PRIMITIVE RITES OF PUBLIC WORSHIP. 199

Prayer—they resound the creed and doxology, and at the end of all the prayers swells the chorus of the "Amen." This made a true service for the people (Λειτουργία), and justified the concluding prayer of thanksgiving: "O God, who hast given us grace with one accord to make these our common supplications unto Thee," etc. These liturgies are also "sacramentaries," *i. e.*, contain orders for the Lord's Supper, assuming it an integral part of a full Christian service.

That, as we have them, they have been elaborated from the simplicity and to some extent from the doctrinal purity of primitive worship, is true. Nevertheless, on the whole, they are rich and precious storehouses of the vital truths of the Gospel, and almost inimitable expressions of the sweetness and power of Christian prayer and praise, and were wonderfully fitted to nourish the spirit of piety on the part of the congregation. And they abide as great historic testimonies of the convictions of the Primitive and Mediæval Church to the value of liturgic usage.

THE REFORMATION AND THE CHURCH SERVICE.

The great religious movement of the sixteenth century was not a work of destruction, but of reformation. And this principle Luther applied to rites and usages as well as to doctrine. Accordingly, in 1523, Luther issued his Order of Public Worship and Communion, which was not a new liturgy, but the historic Church service, pruned of corrupt and redundant ceremonies, so as to be restored to internal harmony with the worship of the Primitive Church. The Latin was displaced by the vernacular of the people. "The sermon has a greatly increased importance, and the purity of doctrine is most carefully guarded; church-song takes a new flight; a few new features are added; but the whole outline and structure of the Western Church for a thousand years before the Reformation are preserved.

"Whatever was pure and scriptural was retained in the old order of parts, and thus the continuity of Christian worship in all centuries and places was kept unbroken. This order of Luther became the basis of all Protestant orders." The universal disposition seems now to be the return to the liturgic use which prevailed immediately after the Reformation, and nothing argues more brightly for the spiritual power and unity of Protestantism.

CHAPTER XXIII.

JOY IN MARTYRDOM. THE CATACOMBS.

IT was characteristic of the sagacious spirit of Imperial Rome, in its world-conquering policy as well as in its religious indifference, to exercise religious toleration. A conquered country, upon its union with the empire, could retain the right to the practice of its distinctive faith and worship.

As illustrative of this broad, liberal spirit, an ancient tradition states that the Emperor Tiberius was so impressed by the report made to him of the scenes attendant on the crucifixion, that he proposed to the senate the enrollment of Christ among the Roman gods and the erection of a statue in his honor.

But two considerations differentiating Christianity from all other religions soon attracted attention and wrought a change in the imperial policy. One was that Christianity claimed not to be a national, or a racial, but a universal religion. It was all-embracing in its scope. Thus it would naturally tend to the subversion of the established Roman religion. The second was, that it asserted itself as *unique*. It was the one only religion. It was the true religion. Others were not merely akin to it as members in the one great family of religions, but were in error, were largely false, were perversions of the faith and worship of the only true and living God.

Hence, the Christians, for conscience sake, refused to do that to which those holding other faiths did not object, viz., to offer incense to the Roman emperors as deities. As religion was intimately interwoven with the Roman state, this refusal was not merely regarded as impious, but as an act of disloyalty. The Roman people, also, were not slow to perceive that the Christians, who had attained the soul enlightenment of the gospel, looked with scorn and derision upon the Pagan images of deities, and regarded their worship as profane, and felt the deepest contempt for the superstitious and absurd rites of the popular religion.

Add to this the tremendous energy of the Christians, the indomitable purpose with which they set about the overthrow of all rival religions, their willingness to endure all sacrifices for their belief, their untiring aggressiveness, and the marvelous

JOY IN MARTYRDOM. THE CATACOMBS. 203

strides with which the new religion was making progress on all sides, and it is not to be wondered at that the Roman rulers took alarm.

PRIMITIVE PERSECUTION OF CHRISTIANS.

So widespread had the Christian faith already become that, in the year 110, Pliny, the Roman governor of Judea, complains to the Emperor Trajan that, owing to the prevalence of this pernicious heresy, the temples and worship of the Roman gods are practically deserted. Feeling, therefore, the necessity of self-preservation, the most energetic measures of repression were taken. It was made unlawful to profess publicly, or to practice the rites of the Christian faith, or to have in keeping the Christian Scriptures.

The first persecution was begun by the Emperor Nero in the year 64. Under Domitian, twenty years later, the property of Christians was confiscated and the professors banished from the empire. Under Trajan, about the year 100, Christian profession was made punishable with death by fire or wild beasts, and thence the horrors of persecution raged with pitiless fury for two long, bloody centuries.

The demeanor of the disciples of the Nazarene prophet under this ordeal has written one of the most glowing chapters in the annals of history. The primitive Christians, taught, no doubt, by our Lord's rebuke of Peter's denial, and by His own unmoved confession before Pontius Pilate, felt that to deny the Lord was an act of unworthy betrayal. They saw, too, that the Roman persecution aimed at the total extermination of Christianity, and that should they prove inconstant, Christianity would fail of its world-saving mission.

We know how human nature shrinks from extraordinary sacrifices, and how the body quivers under excruciating agonies, and hence, no matter how strong their motives, we can never sufficiently wonder at the attitude of this age toward the fiery ordeal of martyrdom.

CONSTANCY OF THE MARTYRS.

Polycarp, the aged bishop of Smyrna, when the prefect besought him, in deference to his great age, to save himself by offering homage to Cæsar, made the heroic answer: " Eighty and six years have I served Him, and He has ever been faithful to me. How, then, can I blaspheme my King and my

Saviour?"* And joyfully he went to the stake, exclaiming : " He will give me strength to endure the fire."

Ignatius, bishop of Antioch, about to be thrown to the lions, so fortifies himself to the test that he looks forward with yearning to so glorious a confession of his crucified Lord. For he counsels the Christians thus: " Pray, then, do not seek to confer any greater favor upon me than that I be sacrificed to God while the altar is still prepared, that being gathered together in love, ye may sing praise." †

Clement holds up these examples for the inspiration of others. " Let us take the noble examples of spiritual heroes furnished in our own generation. The great multitude of the elect, who, having endured extreme indignities and tortures, furnished us with a most excellent example." ‡ And Polycarp characterizes " the chains worn for Christ as the fitting ornaments of saints, and which are, indeed, the diadems of the true elect of God." §

* Epistle of the Church at Smyrna on the Martyrdom of Polycarp, chaps. ix. and xiii.
† Epistle to the Romans, chap. ii.
‡ Epistle to the Romans, chap. ii.
§ Epistle to the Philippians, chap. i.

The refusal to confess Christ, though exposed to severest tortures, was universally deemed treason to the faith, and such were excluded from the communion of the Church. On the other hand, those remaining faithful and escaping with their lives, earned the honorable title "confessors," while those constant unto death attained the illustrious name, "martyrs."

This constancy was illustrated not alone by strong men, but by women and even young and tender girls, as it is recorded of Blandina, that, scourged, her body scorched on a red-hot iron chair, and her limbs torn by wild beasts, her last joyful utterance was the confession, "I die a Christian." So, Perpetua, of noble family, a mother of twenty-two years, with her infant in her arms, and her weeping father enticing her to yield, remained true to the faith, tossed on the horns of a wild cow. The soldier, Basilides, who was charged to immerse the beautiful Potamiæna slowly in boiling pitch, was so moved by her heroic fidelity that he himself embraced Christianity and was beheaded.

PAINTINGS AND INSCRIPTIONS OF THE CATACOMBS.

At a still later period, the catacombs bear thrilling witness to the sufferings and heroism of the primitive martyrs. The catacombs are underground galleries and chambers cut in the soft volcanic rock which abounds in the vicinity of Rome. The passages, if extended in a straight line, would reach for several hundred miles. They are only a few feet wide, so as to make passage possible. These paths and chambers were used at first by the Christians as cemeteries. During the persecutions they were selected as hiding places, as retreats from persecution, and as places where the forbidden worship could be secretly conducted. Bishops were often hidden in these gloomy recesses for years. Tertullian speaks of a "lady unaccustomed to privation, trembling in one of these dark vaults, apprehensive of the capture of her maid, on whom she depends to secretly bring her daily bread."

Great numbers of martyrs were interred in these catacombs, and the inscriptions can still be read. One of the tombs states that five hundred and fifty are therein buried. The inscriptions are most touching, as, " Primitius, in peace, after many torments. A most valiant martyr. His wife erected this to her very sweet and excellent husband." " Here lies Gordeanus, deputy from Gaul, who was martyred for his faith, with all his family. May they rest in peace. Their handmaid, Theophila, made this." The word most frequently found is, Peace. "Being called away, he went in peace." "I'll rest in peace." "Thou dost rest in peace." "He sleeps in hope." "He went to God." "Not lost, but gone before." "*Æterna requies felicitatis*," *i. e.*, "Everlasting rest of happiness." "*In pace decessit*": "He departed in peace."

These inscriptions are in marked contrast to the Pagan ones. On these we find affection and tenderness, but very faint hope. Here are some of them: "I was not, I am, I shall not be." "Here it is. So it is. Nothing else could be." Here I lie in darkness, unhappy girl!" "I lift my hands against the gods, who took me away at the age of twenty, though I had done no harm." "Our hope was in our boy; now all is grief and ashes."

A more striking commentary on the difference between Christianity and merely natural religions could not be found than in the faith and despair contrasted in these epitaphs.

The number of martyrs buried here is very large, noted as running into hundreds of thousands. It is sufficient, at least, to justify the tribute of the

Te Deum; "The noble army of martyrs praise Thee."

We find in these catacombs the earliest instances of Christian art. And the symbolic lessons they teach are very significant as to the spirit of Christianity as interpreted by its confessors of that age. What is remarkable is, that in the face of such hardships and rigors and sufferings, life is not shadowed, but its prevalent tone is that of peace, hope and joy.

PORTRAITS OF CHRIST.

The oldest portrait of Christ is in one of these catacombs, the cemetery of Domitilla—a granddaughter of the Emperor Vespasian. Another is on a sarcophagus of a later period. Both of these portraits are full of dignity and gravity, and the representations of Christ that adhere most faithfully to their expression are superior to later ideal ones.

Jesus is not represented as suffering on the cross or with head crowned with thorns, but as a Shepherd in the bloom of youthful manhood, with a countenance of cheerful, tender grace. Often He is carrying a lamb in His arms. Always He wears a sweet, gentle expression of face. All these pictures are symbols of hope; they suggest faith and comfort. In these gloomy caverns nothing is gloomy. The earliest of the pictures are the brightest, cheeriest, most hopeful of all. The scenes are those of pleasant places. Beautiful grape vines climb over the walls; little birds sit on the branches and peck at the grapes.

There is a picture of the baptism of our Lord in the Jordan. His feet stand in the edge of the river and John the Baptist pours the water from a cup on His head.

Little assurance do Romanists find for some of their cardinal beliefs from these ancient paintings. There are many representations of Peter and Paul. But they are always depicted as equals, sometimes one on one side of Christ and the other on the other. Had the primitive Christians believed in the primacy of Peter we might expect to find at least one representation of our Lord giving the keys to him as head of the Church. But there is no suggestion of the kind. That theological figment has not been discovered at this historic stage. Nor does the Virgin Mary ever appear as receiving extraordinary homage. She is simply depicted as the Virgin Mother holding the Blessed Babe, who

JOY IN MARTYRDOM. THE CATACOMBS. 211

receives the adoration. Instead of receiving prayers, she is herself kneeling in the act of prayer. Nor does the nimbus, an invention of a later theology of superstition, ever appear about her head.

JOYOUSNESS OF EARLY CHRISTIAN ART.

Dean Stanley, after portraying the melancholy and brooding despair shrouding the spirits of the leading Pagans, amid all the beauties of classic literature, and the reveling in opulence and luxury, points to this contrast of the teaching of the mural art of the catacombs: " The graves of these poor sufferers, hid from the public eye in the catacombs, were decorated with an art, rude indeed, yet so triumphant as to make their subterranean squalor radiant with emblems of all that is brightest and most poetic in the happiness of man. While the glimmering taper of the Stoics was burning pale, as though amid the vapors of a charnel-house, the torch of Life, upheld by the hands of the Tarsian tent-maker and the Galilean fisherman had flashed from Damascus to Antioch, from Antioch to Athens, from Athens to Corinth, from Corinth to Ephesus, from Ephesus to Rome." *

* "The Early Days of Christianity," chap. i., p. 10.

And Martineau speaks thus eloquently : "There the evergreen leaf protests in sculptural silence that the winter of the grave cannot touch the saintly soul, the blossoming branch speaks of vernal suns beyond the snows of this chill world ; the good shepherd shows from his benign looks that the mortal way, so terrible to nature, had become to those Christians as the meadow-path between the grassy slopes and beside the still waters." *

A wonderful illustration, sorely needed in our era of an ease and luxury that often tend to materialism and effeminacy of character, is the fortitude here shown, illustrative of that Scripture : "This is the victory that overcometh the world, even your faith." † There we learn how far the soul is stronger than the body, and how the immaterial element in man can triumph over the mightiest outward forces. And how faith can so strengthen itself in the divine as to meet all earthly perils and powers with patience, and even with a masterful joy.

It even came to be regarded as so sure a test of Christian fidelity, and to be felt that the noble confession made by martyrdom would bring into so

* "Hours of Thought," p. 155. † 1 John v. 4.

much more intimate a relation with the Lord, that despite the crucible of anguish, it was sought with gladness. The courage of Christians grew stronger in the midst of dangers and horrors. "An enthusiasm for martyrdom sprang up, a desire to win an eternal heaven through a few hours of suffering. Martyrdom came to be believed to be the surest road to heaven, better than all good works. The Christians offered themselves to die—seeking persecutions, glorying in shame." "These tortures," said St. Basil, "so far from being a terror, are rather a pleasure." "Kill us, rack us, grind us to powder," says Tertullian, "our numbers increase in proportion as you mow us down." *

Undoubtedly, the apostolic fathers did believe that constancy to a good confession brought a special reward, yet there is manifest no visionary or intemperate enthusiasm in their conception. Thus, Clement speaks "of the noble steadfastness of the martyrs, and of the striking example of patience" † given by their firmness. And Hermas gives this incitement to fidelity: "All who have suffered for the name of the Lord are honorable be-

* "Events and Epochs in Religious History," Clarke, p. 19.
† First Epistle, chap. v.

fore God. Ye who suffer for His name ought to glorify God because He deemed you worthy to bear His name, that all your sins might be remitted." *
And, following in the line of our Lord's promise to James and John, if they should be baptized with His baptism, it is said that those "who have borne scourges, prisons, crosses, wild beasts, great tribulations for God's name's sake, shall sit on God's right hand." But, then, to show the sober scriptural view of the writer, it is added, "But both for those who sit on the right, and for those who sit on the left, there are the same gifts and promises." †

A GLORIOUS EPOCH OF CHRISTIAN HISTORY.

The unflinching courage of the Christians of this primitive age, and their endurance of martyrdom in its extremest form in an era of barbaric cruelty, constitute not only the most glorious epoch in Christianity, but in the history of our race. Many sad and degrading things have made the annals of mankind often a most humiliating one, but here we see it transfigured with a splendor that glorifies our common humanity.

* " Pastor of Hermas," Book III., " Similitude," IX.
† Ibid., Book I., Vision III., chap. ii.

We see, with all the lack of appreciation for it, what a priceless treasure religion is to the soul that realizes its value, and what it will sacrifice and endure before it will abjure its unspeakable hope. We learn, too, the power of the Christian faith. The adherents of heathen religions have, too, been willing to die for their beliefs, but never would they have the settled, patient strength of conviction to endure, as did the early Christians, the power of raging, all-powerful persecution for century after century. And this faith at last exhausted all the resources of the persecutors. The blood of the martyrs only became the seed of the Church. And when the last of the Pagan emperors, Julian, saw the final collapse of the resort to bloody force, and dying, exclaimed, "*Tandem vicisti Galilæe !*"— "At length thou hast conquered, O Galilean!" The victory of Christianity was complete.

As was the fierceness of the trial of the early believers, such was their invisible help. And, as the disciples who witnessed the martyrdom of their beloved bishop, Polycarp, thought they saw the fire, instead of burning his body, shaping itself into an arch about him, so that it but shed a golden halo upon his person, so may we believe that, as her visions came again to Joan of Arc when the flames burst about her, the ascended Lord was with the saints in spirit, if not in vision, to strengthen them until, the fiery crucible over and the victory won, they received their heavenly crown.

The constancy of the martyrs has shown the invincibility of the soul stayed on Christ, and the indestructibility of the Christian Church. It excited the wonder of the Pagans; it silenced the mockery of infidels; it convinced the serious inquirers of the supernatural sanction of the religion of Jesus. It will forever be the heroic age to which Christians, amid new perils to the faith, can return for a new birth of that devotion and courage which will enable them to evince a no less unshaken constancy and to win a no less memorable victory.

CHAPTER XXIV.

EDUCATIONAL RELIGIOUS METHODS. THE EARLY CHURCH AND CHRISTIAN NURTURE.

THE qualities equal to times that try men's souls are not of sudden growth. Patience is not born in a night. Courage and endurance are the results of a process. Character, that has issued from the formative forces of instruction and experience, can alone withstand the severe onsets of temptation. The vessel most carefully constructed, whose hull has been fitted by painstaking preparation to meet coming shocks, though later in launching, will most safely ride the dangers of the deep.

This principle was well understood by the early Christians. There was no use in hastily-made converts. They could not afford to resort to emotional methods. Such additions would be but a source of weakness. Those who, like the seed sown on the rock would hastily spring up, but for lack of root in time of temptation fall away, would only weaken the cause. Disciples must be well grounded in their profession. Their convictions must be deep in order to hold. Their confidence must be rational to meet the challenges it must encounter. To make answer for the faith that is in them, their beliefs must be intelligently embraced. To overcome in so hot a warfare, they must be armed with the whole panoply of defence. Not to lose heart under trial, they must have given proof of deep, genuine and thorough spiritual renewal.

THE CATECHUMENATE.

Hence, the methods of the primitive period were adapted to effect these solid results. The greatest care was exercised in the reception of members. Adults and youth of an understanding age were divided into two or three classes, in which they underwent a course of thorough instruction. "The Church was profoundly earnest in its preparation. The more sensible the ancient Church was of the fact that merely nominal Christians intruded themselves too often into the communion of the Church, the more seriously did it occupy itself with the catechumens. From the beginning of the second century, such as sought to be incorporated into the Church received, under the title of catechumens, preliminary instruction from a teacher expressly appointed for the purpose. The whole period of their probation lasted two years." *

The Apostolical Constitutions make the course three years. This passage will show the caution exercised in the admission of candidates: " Those that first come to the mystery of godliness, let them be brought to the minister by the deacons, and let them be examined as to the causes wherefor they are come to the Word of the Lord. And let those that bring them inquire exactly about their character, and give them their testimony. Let their previous manners and lives be inquired into [to find that they are tolerating no action or habit incompatible with a religious profession]. Let him who is to be a catechumen be a catechumen for three years. Any candidate who is diligent and has a good will to his business shall be admitted. Let him that teaches be skillful in the Word and grave in his manners, for they shall be all taught of God." †

The catechumens were instructed in the Scriptures and in the meaning and significance of the

---

* Guericke's " Christian Antiquities," sec. 31.
† " Constitutions of the Holy Apostles," Book VIII., chap. xxxii.

sacraments, and in the Creed, which, at that period, was transmitted not by writing but by word of mouth. Before baptism, a definite and positive profession of faith was demanded in the formulary prescribed by the Church. At the same time, there was a careful examination conducted as to their fitness. In connection with the baptism, after the precedent of the Apostolical practice (Acts viii. 16, 17), it was customary to bless by the imposition of hands as a sign of religious consecration, and also of the gift of the Holy Spirit.

CONFIRMATION AND CHRISTIAN NURTURE.

At a later period this rite, in view of the prevalence of Infant Baptism, was separated from Baptism, and called Confirmation. It then became the ceremony by which baptized children, having reached years of intelligent decision, made their public profession of faith, were received into full communion with the Church, and admitted to participation of the Lord's Supper. This they were only permitted to do after a thorough curriculum of study under the pastor or skilled lay teacher.

It was one of the greatest evils in the degeneracy of the middle ages that this intelligent instruction of candidates for Church membership had fallen into disuse, and that, accordingly, gross ignorance prevailed among Christians on the essential doctrines of Christianity. Luther, to remedy this, prepared his Catechism, in which, by means of a system of questions and answers, he expounds, as he says, in a simple manner, "such as it should be taught by the head of a family," the Ten Commandments, or divine law; the Creed, or the plan of redemption; the Lord's Prayer; and the sacraments of Baptism and the Lord's Supper. Added to lessons in this Catechism were instruction in the Bible, in Church History, in the Church Confessions, etc., so that the candidates for confirmation were thoroughly grounded in the essential doctrines of the faith they were to profess.

This idea of Christian nurture harmonizes with that of the ancient Church. It is that the child by baptism is received into the covenant. It is now a member of the kingdom of God, baptized not alone with water but with the Holy Ghost. By this act God has sealed it to Himself, and has implanted within it the seed of regeneration. Its sanctification is now a process of growth. There is to be no sudden conversion, no violent transition from the world to God, no startling or revolutionary religious experience. But, through Christian nurture, the child is to progress in the new life, daily growing stronger, and bearing maturer fruits of grace. By this process, it passes naturally to the stage of confirmation, and, well-grounded and prepared, enters into full church communion. This is the true conception of the position of a child of Christian parents, instead of the view which would consider it out of Christ, out of the kingdom, and out of the reach of salvation, until, in later years, by a sudden conversion it is admitted to the number of the saved.

RELIGIOUS EDUCATION.

This is the theory of Christian nurture based upon the educational system, and we believe it to be built upon the teachings of Scripture and sustained by the soundest principles of pedagogy, as it is upheld by the experience and history of the Church. And it is, we think, to be regretted that this judicious system has to so large an extent been deserted by modern practice for that of the revivalistic method. As compared with the latter, a late number of the *Reformed Church Review* remarks on a new edition of Luther's catechetical writings:

"Since the American churches have for more

than a century forsaken the educational system of religion and have largely surrendered their heritage to revivalism, we consider this publication most timely. It sets forth clearly the interdependence of religion and education. Christianity is to appeal to the intellect and conscience, and to mold the mind and heart. It is not a mere momentary experience, a passing ecstasy, or a sporadic emotion. It is a life which is begotten by the Spirit of God through His Word. It is nourished by Christian instruction in the home, the school and the congregation. It is sustained by the sacraments and Christian fellowship. In this way only will the churches develop a normal Christian manhood, increase the number and holiness of their members, and extend their borders to the ends of the earth."

Many of the principles of religious pedagogy, which are now proclaimed as new discoveries, are only rediscoveries of original Protestant ideals which were held alike by the reformers of the Lutheran and Reformed churches. While no one will deny that great progress has been made in the understanding of the child mind and in the preparation of juvenile literature, we must not forget that the Reformers were the fathers of these movements. In a sense, we can go forward only by going backward to their principles, though we would not be forever bound by their forms.

MODERN EVANGELISTIC METHODS.

It is sometimes argued that the outpouring of the Holy Ghost on the Day of Pentecost, and the conversion of three thousand souls, is an example countenancing the modern revivalistic idea of a sudden accession of large numbers. But assuredly there is nothing analogous in the cases. A very different method is necessary for the founding of a Church from that required for its continuance. That was, as the occasion demanded, a supernatural outpouring of the Holy Spirit; now we have emerged from the miraculous period, and the gift of the Spirit is in accordance with the natural order.

Our Lord's teaching is certainly the true guide here. He represented the descent of the Spirit as silent and imperceptible. "Thou canst not tell whence it cometh and whither it goeth; so is everyone that is born of the Spirit." * The noise and publicity and demonstration and spectacular methods necessary to a revivalistic campaign are

* John iii. 7.

anything but favorable to the deep, silent, powerful working of the Spirit, as our Lord here portrays it. It is not amid such scenes that the soul hears "the still small voice." Further, our Lord likens the general work of religion on the spirit to a growth : " First the blade, then the ear, after that the full corn in the ear." * Here we have outlined most forcibly the idea of Christian nurture. And Christ ever insisted on faith, which is an energy of the will, instead of feeling, which is an energy of the heart.

Every thoughtful consideration, then, gives the preference to the ancient and historic method of making religious converts. The modern method prevalent in many quarters is emotional instead of educational. It makes religion a matter of feeling and impulse instead of intelligent and deliberate action. Consequently, with the subsidence of the impulse dies the resolve. The reaction is most hurtful, if not fatal, to the religious sense. As Phillips Brooks wrote : " After the fever comes the chill."

It prompts to reliance on special instead of regular effort. But the religious life is supported by the

* Mark iv. 28.

constant and orderly application of means. When a church loses faith in its regular agencies and depends for divine visitations on special and exceptional efforts, it foregoes its chief and normal source of strength. It brings into prominence the individual instead of the Word of God. The regular preacher, through his ordinary ministrations, cannot win souls, but some remarkably endowed personality is charged with that extraordinary spiritual power. Thereby the human instrumentality is exalted to the depreciation of the divine. But our faith is not to stand " in the wisdom of men, but in the power of God."

REGULAR AND ORDERLY RELIGIOUS AGENCIES.

The practice of the primitive Church in this respect is most significant. As it was some time before all the churches could be provided with a regular ministry, teachers—variously called apostles or prophets—made tours of the congregations, instructing them in the Gospel. But, not only was the greatest care exercised to see that they be thoroughly equipped and pure in doctrine, but they were only entertained as guests, and not permitted to make but the briefest stay.

The Didache (Teaching of the Twelve Apostles) gives these guarded directions respecting such evangelistic visitors: "Whosoever, therefore, cometh and teacheth you all these things that have been taught before, receive him. But concerning the apostles and prophets, according to the decree of the Gospel, thus do. Let every Apostle [Gospel messenger] that cometh to you be received as the Lord. But he shall not remain but one day; but if there be need, also the next; but if he remain three days he is a false prophet. And when the Apostle goeth away, let him take nothing but bread until he lodgeth, but if he ask money, he is a false prophet."* It is evident that such a rule would reduce quite materially the number of modern professional evangelists. They would find themselves urgently called to some other business. So jealously did the early Church guard the prerogatives of the settled ministry from the occasional religious itinerant.

Once more, the revivalistic method depreciates the Church and its order. Its special function is the saving of souls. It is not merely a home to which those are to resort who have been saved by some other way. The divine order is that the Holy

* Didache, chap. xi.

Spirit is not given immediately, but mediately. The new birth is to be mediated by Word and Sacrament. It is to be attained through the Means of Grace. The Means are not to be used as a secondary thing after conversion. But they are the instruments by which it is to be wrought. Hence, the divine order is inverted and the whole plan of grace confused and totally misconceived by the revival method. How can fruitful and enduring results in soul birth and religious culture be expected from work conducted on such unscriptural and injudicious pedagogical principles.

Accordingly, it is noteworthy that the churches pursuing the historic educational method are the growing churches. Their accessions may not at any one time be so large, but they are regular and constant. They may not be demonstrative or attract so much public attention, but they are lasting. We conclude with the view lately expressed by Rev. Dr. Charles E. Jefferson: "The Church has never made lasting conquests, except where it has used the interlocutory method of instruction. Instruction—painstaking, continuous, systematic instruction—this is the crying need of the Christian Church in our day."

CHAPTER XXV.

THE END OF THE WORLD—OTHER-WORLDLINESS.

GIBBON utters the taunt with respect to the sub-apostolic time that the believers were so busily preparing themselves in heavenly virtues for the expected coming of Christ that "It was not in this world that the primitive Christians were desirous of making themselves useful. They were not less averse to the business than to the pleasures of this world." * Yet then, on the next page, he shows that "this contempt of the world" "exercised them in the habits of humility, meekness and patience," "inured them to chastity, temperance, economy and all the domestic virtues," prompted them to unselfishness and charity, and kept them from any acts "disturbing the public peace of society." It would be hard to specify qualities constituting more valuable citizens and more desirable neighbors.

The fact that their lives were in such pointed

---

* "Decline and Fall of the Roman Empire," Vol. I., chap. xv.

contrast to the immorality and pitiless selfishness of the surrounding Pagans, certainly shows that the love of their fellow-men and the desire to be useful were animating and dominant purposes. The taunt is one that has often been made against a spiritual-minded society, and with as little ground.

The early Christians did, indeed, look for the coming end of the world. Thus writes Clement: "Of a truth, soon and suddenly shall His will be accomplished, as the Scripture also bears witness: 'the Lord shall suddenly come to His temple, even the Holy One.'"* As the prophecy of Malachi in which this prophecy of Christ's speedy coming to end the world had already been delayed for five hundred years, we can understand with what caution as to undue expectation Clement here applies it.

Again, Polycarp writes: "He comes as the Judge of the quick and the dead."† Whereupon he follows this warning with an exhortation to "forgive and it shall be forgiven you; be merciful and ye shall obtain mercy," and to the practice of those virtues of love and gentleness and patience, which banish the asperities and enhance the sweetness of

* Epistle of Clement, chap. xxiii.
† Epistle to the Philippians, chap. ii.

life. Ignatius: "He also died and rose again and ascended into the heavens to Him that sent Him, and is set down at His right hand, and shall come at the end of the world, with His Father's glory, to judge the living and the dead, and to render to everyone according to his works."*

No stronger allusions to the end of the world than these are made in any of their works. It is noticeable that these references are chiefly in Christ's own words, and refer as much to His glory as to their importance as warnings. They are marked by strength and dignity, and are no more declarative and emphatic than the Church's confession of the second coming made in the ecumenical creeds to-day. Nowhere is there the slightest intimation that the primitive Christians looked for such a speedy coming of the end of all things as to loosen their hold on the present, or relax their interest in the instant duties of life.

There is not a particle of evidence that extravagant views on the *Parousia* were held. There is no fanatical assembling on some mountain-top, like the Millerites, arrayed in white robes, expecting the Lord's sudden descent. They only held, as Christ

* Epistle to the Magnesians, chap. xiii.

meant believers to hold, that His second coming and the end of the world impended over every age, and that they should ever " be looking and hasting unto the coming of the day of the Lord." *

That is, they viewed life under the aspect of eternity. And this but gave it a vaster scope, and clothed it with a greater grandeur.

ONLY SINFUL PLEASURES SHUNNED.

That they largely kept aloof from participation in the pleasures of the age was owing to the natural tendency of every time for excess in these, but also especially to the fact that these pleasures were in the hands of the heathen, and could not be entered into without sharing the immoral vices with which they were associated.

It is only sinful pleasures against which they warn. As Clement: " Seeing, therefore, that we are the portion of the Holy One, let us do all those things which pertain to holiness, avoiding all evil speaking, all impure embraces, together with drunkenness and execrable pride. But moderation, humility and meekness belong to such as are blessed by Him." †

* 2 Peter iii. 12. † First Epistle, chap. xxx.

Similarly, they largely abstained from business for the most valid reasons. They could hold no public office, or be members of the Roman senate, for each member, on taking his seat, was required to offer incense at the Pagan altar. And acts of similar idolatry were connected with banquets and festivals, so that they could not consistently take part in them.

For Christians thus to live in a dominant heathen society, where there was such a contrariety in all their beliefs, principles and motives of conduct, was a most difficult thing. And to maintain their Christian character and to gain respect and influence for the faith they professed, it was absolutely necessary that they keep themselves from compromising associations.

But, further than this, they did not stand aloof. They exhibited no fanatical indifference to earthly tasks and human interests. A remarkable proof of this is their repudiation of Montanism. The Montanists did seek to have Christians maintain an exclusive attitude to the heathen and to lead lives of the severest rigor and to have the Church exercise the strictest discipline in view of the near coming of Christ, but the judicious common sense of Christians condemned this sect as extreme. " By the condemnation and expulsion of Montanism, in which the inner development of the Post-Apostolic Age reached its special and distinctive conclusion, the endeavor to naturalize Christianity among the social customs of the worldly life was certainly legitimized by the Church, and could now be unrestrictedly carried out in a wider and more comprehensive way." *

PRIMITIVE PIETY NOT ASCETIC OR SINGULAR.

The Epistle to Diognetus defines the primitive position in these significant terms : " For the Christians are distinguished from other men neither by country, nor language, nor the customs which they observe. They do not lead a life which is marked out by any singularity. But, inhabiting Greek as well as barbarian cities, according as the lot of each of them has determined, and following the customs of the natives in respect to language, clothing, food and the rest of their ordinary conduct, they display their confessedly wonderful method of life. They are in the flesh, but they do not live after the flesh. They pass their days on earth, but they are citizens of heaven. They obey the prescribed laws, and, at

* Kurtz's " Church History," Vol. I., p. 73.

the same time, surpass the laws by their lives. They love all men and are persecuted by all. They are poor, yet make many rich." *

A finer portraiture than this of the Christian character could not be painted. It is in perfect harmony with our Lord's charge to His disciples that they should not be taken "out of the world" and "yet not be of the world." † And with St. Paul's counsel, to "use the world as not abusing it." ‡ In short, they illustrated that acute thought of Charles Kingsley as to the large and discreet wisdom with which Christians view worldly things: "None know less of the world than those who pride themselves on being men of the world. For the true light, which shines all around them, they do not see, and therefore they do not see the truth of things of the light." §

There was no asceticism in the manners of the primitive Christians. Their lives showed an equal balance between temporal pleasures on the one hand and a one-sided spirituality on the other. Their other-worldliness was of a true type. They led

* Epistle to Diognetus, chap. v.
† John xvii. 16.   ‡ 1 Cor. vii. 31.
§ "Truths from Kingsley," p. 91.

holy lives, evincing to all that their minds were not immersed in temporal pleasures, but that while they enjoyed with thankful hearts the good things of life, they were "seekers for a city that hath foundations, whose builder and maker is God."

They associated freely with unbelievers that their faith and piety and hope might be a leaven to regenerate and save them. But in so doing, they took good care that the reproach could not be cast upon them that they worshiped Mammon, and sought as eagerly after perishing prizes as did the surrounding Pagans.

In short, their other-worldliness was one of the most unanswerable arguments and one of the loudest sermons in favor of Christianity. And if believers to-day only illustrated the same ideals, it would take away much reproach from the Church and mightily tend to win the world to Christ.

CHAPTER XXVI.

THE APOSTOLIC FATHERS AND THE FUTURE STATE.

THE apostolic fathers lived in an environment of gloom with respect to the future. The greater the thinker the deeper were his misgivings and doubts. Life, to the vision penetrating into the heart of it, and taking into account its hopeless end, was esteemed rather a tragedy than a blessing.

The symbols by which the Pagan writers described man were those of sadness without hope. To Homer they were a generation of "leaves," to Pindar a "shadowy dream," to Æschylus "phantoms" passing away. Sophocles, in the "Œdipus," thus bewails their fate: "Happiest never to have been born, and never to see the piercing rays of the sun; and for one who is born soon to pass through the gates of Hades, and to lie deep under the earth." These were the bitter refrains of an earlier Pagan time, but that no further light had been gained since the era of Homer and Socrates is shown by the saying of Pliny: "Many have thought it the best lot never to have been born, or to have died very speedily," and the sentiment of Plutarch:

" Come, O death, thou true physician for all our ills ;
 Thou heaven, that shelterest man from the storm of pain."

The deep notes of subdued despair which sound from the innermost hearts of these writers show what a crushing burden it is to thinkers brooding over the deepest problems of life to contemplate the black abyss of the extinction of being.

But in what a different realm of thought do we find ourselves when we look into these early Christian writers. Nothing can give us a more vivid glimpse of the revolution on this darkest question of the ages inaugurated by the teachings of Jesus. Here life wears the glow of eternity. Death has been abolished. The grave has lost its gloom. All over the mysteries and crosses and sorrows of life arches the rainbow of hope. We have passed from darkness to light, from defeat to victory, from wails of despair to songs of triumph. The transit from the Pagan to the Christian era is as the entrance upon another world.

Polycarp: "If we please God in this present world, we shall receive also the future world, according as Christ has promised that He will raise us again, and that if we live worthily of Him, we shall also reign together with Him." *

IMMORTALITY AND BODILY RESURRECTION.

Immortality is assumed as settled beyond question.

Nor is the future state to be that of a disembodied spiritual existence. Clement: "Let us consider, beloved, how the Lord continually proves to us that there shall be a future resurrection, of which He has rendered the Lord Jesus Christ the firstfruits by raising Him from the dead." † "For I know," says Ignatius, "that after His resurrection Christ was still in the flesh, and I believe Him to be so now, for after His resurrection He did eat and drink with them." ‡ Not, then, was this life to be that hoped for by the ancients, where the unhappy shades bewail the loss of those senses which gave zest to existence. But as the soul was to live, so was the body to rise. And, though it was to be changed, yet this change was not to take from it the qualities of body. Though, then, it is to be a spiritual as against a natural, it is none the

* Epistle, chap. v. † First Epistle, chap. xxiv.
‡ Epistle to Trallians, chap. ix.

less to be a real body, instrument and servant of the spirit.

Their view is in harmony with that of Martensen: "When we speak of the resurrection of the body, or of the flesh, we do not mean literally those sensible materials making up our present frame, which in this life even are in a continual state of change, and are continually vanishing; we mean the eternal and ideal form (not τὸ υλικόν, but τὸ εἶδος, as Origen says); and we acknowledge, at the same time, the essential identity of that new body with the earthly tabernacle in which we dwell during this temporal life; that it will not be another, but the same corporeal individuality which shall be raised again and glorified, according to its ideal." *

CHRIST'S RESURRECTION REAL.

This assurance of resurrection and immortality was based upon the belief in the Lord's resurrection. That was held to be a literal fact. Our Lord arose from the dead with a true body, and this identical, —though so changed and spiritualized as to be "glorified,"—with the one He had worn on earth, even to bearing the wounds made on the cross. It

* "Christian Dogmatics," sec. 275.

was this crowning miracle that certified the divinity of Christ, and gave boldness to the apostolic message, even as St. Paul affirms that "Jesus Christ was declared to be the Son of God with power by the resurrection from the dead." *

The claim of rationalistic thought, even within the Christian Church in the present day, is that the apostles were deceived, their heated imaginations creating a delusive vision of the Christ, or, as Walker suggests—while he holds to the reality of the resurrection—that it was only an apparitional manifestation. †

Yet all admit the fundamental place the fact of the resurrection held in primitive Christianity. Without the belief in it, there would have been no proclamation of the gospel. "It is undeniable," says Schmiedel, "that the Church was founded, not directly upon the fact of His resurrection, but upon a belief in His resurrection, and this faith worked with equal power whether the resurrection was an actual fact or not."

And Harnack admits: "Whatever may have happened at the grave, and in the matter of appear-

* Rom. i. 4.
† "Christian Theism and a Spiritual Monism," p. 408.

ances, one thing is certain, this grave was the birthplace of the indestructible belief that death is vanquished; that there is life eternal." *

There is no need for strained hypotheses and subtle evasions here. Christianity is based upon historical facts. Its evidences are realities, not illusions. It is altogether irrational and incredible that the religion which gives every sign of being the one true, absolute religion should be built upon a myth. "Why should it be thought a thing incredible that God should raise the dead?" There is nothing in the New Testament so thoroughly substantiated by impartial criticism as the belief of the apostles in the reality of Christ's resurrection. As yet there has been suggested no way of accounting for that belief so satisfactory as the hypothesis that the apostles actually experienced what they thought they experienced.

"Take away the historical, risen Jesus and you take away the Gospel in its original sense. And you change the definition of Christianity itself. The facts on which the Gospel was based were objective." †

* "Essence of Christianity," p. 162.
† "The Church and the Changing Order," Shailer **Matthews**, p. 62.

Historicity is an essential characteristic of the Gospel. It is built upon a revelation of objective facts. The crowning one of these is the true bodily resurrection of Jesus Christ. Why should one who professes to receive Christianity deny it?

This veritable resurrection, in a changed but identical form, of the earthly body, bore with it a perpetuation of the experiences, reminiscences and endearments of the earthly stage. And yet, "glorified," after the fashion of Christ's risen body, it is to be endowed with new attributes of incorruptibility, painlessness, and a vast enlargement of powers.

STATE OF THE HOLY DEAD.

The future life, too, was to be one in the kingdom and presence of God. The saints were to reign with their ascended King, and life to be one eternally progressive scale of holiness, rapture and glory. It was thus to fulfill the Saviour's significant promise: "I am come that they might have life, and that they might have it more abundantly." *

According to the Reliques of the Elders, preserved in Irenæus, V., 36, there were to be different

* John x. 10.

degrees of reward in this one heaven of happiness. "As the Elders say, then also shall they which have been deemed worthy of the abode in heaven go thither, while others shall enjoy the delight of Paradise, and others again shall possess the brightness of the city, *for in every place the Saviour shall be seen*, according as they be worthy who see Him." *

No wonder, then, that in this larger, transfigured view of the existence to come the grave was robbed of its sting, and death swallowed up in victory, so that, though he must pass the testing ordeal of martyrdom to reach it, Ignatius, in prison, entreats his friends not to seek to prevent his departure, saying: "I shall willingly die for God, unless He hinder me. Suffer me to become food for the wild beasts, through whose instrumentality it will be granted me to attain to God. But, when I suffer, I shall become the freedman of Jesus, and shall rise again, emancipated by Him. Pardon me, I know what is for my benefit." †

THE FUTURE STATE FIXED AND ETERNAL.

The future state, for our patristic writers, is not,

* Cited in Lightfoot's "Apostolic Fathers," p. 562.
† Epistle to the Romans.

however, without its dread responsibilities and stern realities. They look forward to a general judgment, and to a separation between the righteous and the wicked. And these diverse states they hold to be everlasting. Barnabas writes: "But the way of darkness is also the way of everlasting death, with punishment, in which way are the things that destroy the soul." * Clement: "For if we do the will of Christ we shall find rest, otherwise nothing shall deliver us from eternal punishment." † Polycarp answers to the threat of the Roman Proconsul: "Thou threatenest me with fire which burneth for an hour, and after a little is extinguished, but art ignorant of the fire of the coming judgment and of eternal punishment, reserved for the ungodly." ‡

The state of the dead, subsequent to the General Judgment, is here seen to be fixed. Time is the sphere of probation, that of eternity the era of irrevocable condition.

IS THERE FOR SOME A SECOND PROBATION?

There is, however, difference of view as to a second probation between death and the judgment.

* Epistle, chap. xx. † Epistle, chap. viii.
‡ Encyclical Epistle of the Church at Smyrna, chap. xi.

Clement states: "But after that we have departed from the world, we shall no longer then be able to confess, or to exercise repentance." * But Hermas has this remarkable passage: "If any of Christ's elect sin after a certain day which has been fixed, he shall not be saved. For the repentance of the righteous has limits. Filled up are the days of repentance to all the saints; but to the heathen repentance will be possible even to the last day." † The reconciliation of these seemingly diverse statements, no doubt, is found in this, that Clement speaks only of those enlightened, and Hermas equally excludes them from a future repentance. While Hermas's further assertion of an opportunity to be given the heathen in the future, and before the General Judgment to have Christ preached for their acceptance or rejection, is one of the most important utterances we find in the fathers.

As to the intermediate state—the souls of the dead awaiting the resurrection—that which has sometimes been called after Scripture imagery a sleep, which, however, cannot be taken in a strictly literal sense,—as it evidently implies no more than a state of quiet review of the past and of profound

* Epistle, chap. viii. † Vision II., chap. ii.

self-fathoming,—the lives of the fathers seem to have been too strenuously occupied with the realities of the present to have given thought to it.

THE GREAT FUTURE HOPE.

Although, then, their views of the future state are set on the dark background of the divine necessity of a distinction between sin and righteousness, and between an evil and a well-spent life, and of an eternal separation between the two, yet they are convictions of assurance and hope. They make being in time not a shadow, but a substance. Life is not the sport of a pitiless fate, but the guarded child of an Almighty Father. The future is not a shroud of gloom, but a clothing upon with a new and more glorious life.

In fact, in their view of the blessedness of the coming state, the brightness of that heavenly existence illumines even the deepest sorrows and darkest passages of the life on earth with a prophetic splendor. Professor Woodberry, in his "Great Writers,"* calls attention to the strains of triumph and hope in the early Christian literature at about the same time that Virgil was writing his immortal

* "Critique on Virgil," pp. 136-140.

poem, the "Æneid," breathing the spirit of pitilessness and struggle and defeat and suffering, which reflected the despairing temper of the ancient world—as vividly seen in Æneas, even in the Elysian fields, marveling why any soul should desire to see the light of life.

"Pain, pain, ever, forever," rings through the "Æneid" like a Promethean cry. So does the greatest poem of the Pagan world, expressing the temper of the mightiest race of antiquity, present its contrast of pain and despair with the tranquillity and faith and joy which shine on the pages illumed by the great future hope.

CHAPTER XXVII.

THE OLD FAITH AND THE "NEW THEOLOGY."

IN nature we find two determining forces, the fixed and the variable, the settled and the changing. The laws, the forces, the substance, are and abide the same. The phenomena are variable. The former feature gives nature its solidity and security, the latter clothes it with the diverse forms of beauty. The same principle holds true in the realm of thought. There are basic truths which are settled forever. Upon the immovability of these alone is built the ever-shifting scenery of thought. Shake or unsettle these fixed foundations and the whole intellectual structure falls.

The *new* has a wonderful charm for the human mind. Man is vigorous and alert, and presses on to every new field of discovery with unabated ardor. This progressive spirit is the noblest attribute of the mind, and to it we are indebted for the great and beneficent advances that have been made in knowledge and happiness in the course of history. And it is the glory of our modern time that this spirit of pressing on to the new and unknown is everywhere rife. Yet we must be on our guard that it be not a one-sided movement. That it do not forget the rock whence it is hewn and on which it stands.

Progress, it must ever be remembered, is a resultant of these centrifugal and centripetal thought forces. The one must hold it to the center, must bind it to the universal order, if the propelling force is not to plunge all into chaos. Thus correlated there will be an orderly and beneficent advance. True progress must ever have its feet fixed upon the past, while its face is towards the future.

EVERY AGE NEEDS A NEW THEOLOGY.

These axiomatic truths have their highest application with respect to religion. Hence it is justly held that, on the one hand, we must persevere and stand fast in the Old Faith, while our age needs a new theology, as does every age. The Old Faith, " once delivered to the saints " is of God, is divine, is of absolute and eternal authority. But it must be stated in modern terms, in the categories of present-day thought, and must be adapted to the phases and experiences and problems and needs of the time.

It is a caricature of orthodox conservatives to assert that they expect the theology of to-day to be identical with the theology of the past. Only its fundamental principle must abide that it forms itself by the substance of the divine revelation. Its concrete expression must ever be regulated by and in adaptation to the thought, knowledge, science, problems, temptations and living conditions of to-day. "The Church must preach some form of theology, and theology, in the first analysis, is the result of the effort of thinkers of an age to correlate the facts of religion with the other facts they see." *
Hence, Christian Theology must be progressive and have a history, as it, in fact, has.

But the substance of the faith must not be changed in the theological crucible. For it is alone in its basal invariability that lies its claim to be absolute truth, and that consists its power to assure and satisfy the soul. It is "the same yesterday, to-day and forever." The faith that has been confessed in the primitive, mediæval and modern age, that has stood immutable amid all the fluctuations of the human stage, is that in which men alone

* "The Church and the Changing Order," Shailer Matthews, p. 13.

will be ready to trust the everlasting welfare of their souls. Contrariwise, a religion whose teachings would shift with every flutter of the vane of transient thought, never has gained and never will command the serious attention of men.

In accord with these principles we find that, while the cardinal truths of the Gospel were presented in germinal purity in the writers of this sub-New Testament era, we to-day stand far ahead of them, both in our fuller appreciation of their significance and in the clear, philosophic conception and statement of them. All truth is endowed with life, and growth is an unfailing trait of life. Especially is this so of the great Christian truths. "My words are spirit, and they are life," said Jesus. The Word of God is not only a seed to fructify in the heart, but to gather increase of light and power and wonder in the mind.

THEOLOGY A PROGRESSIVE SCIENCE.

So the intellects of acute Christian thinkers have developed nobler systems of truth on the basis of the Gospel in every age. Especially as these truths came into conflict with error were they more exactly apprehended and more accurately set forth in the Church's historic confessions. Or, as these beliefs were subjected to the test of persecution were they fashioned in the crucible of experience to a finer, purer and more durable texture. Forrest, in the "Christ of History and Experience," thus shows how those carefully framed definitions, to which loosely girded thinkers take objection, were forced upon the Church by polemical assaults and were absolutely essential to the defence and preservation of the Christian system. Thus, in the adoption of the Nicene Creed, there was a notable advance as to the Trinity; in the era of Augustine a far clearer and more helpful statement of the doctrines of sin and grace; in Luther's time the most evangelical unfolding of the saving truth of justification by faith; while Dr. Dorner's great work on the "Person of Christ" marks an acuter insight into the deep question of the union of the divine and human natures in the God-Man, Christ Jesus. The office of a true theology, as John Stuart Mill says of philosophy, "is not to set aside old definitions, but it corrects and regulates them."

But this progress has not been, as many would now claim, negative, but positive. It has not been an advance by demolition, but by conservation and construction. It has not diminished and weakened the edifice of Christianity, but enlarged and fortified it. It has added to the body of the faith, not decreased it. It has given a vast enrichment to Christian theology, not undermined and denuded it. That is not progress which destroys the pillars supporting it and cuts away the foundations on which it rests. But that alone is progress worthy the name which retains and conserves each past gain, and builds upon a structure ever rising higher and ever gathering larger proportions of strength and majesty. Or, as Ruskin puts it : " The generations as they pass do not carve their work in snow that will melt, but are rolling a great, white, gathering snow-ball—higher and higher, larger and larger—along the Alps of human power."

Such has been the advance of theology. Its progress has not been by subtraction, by paring down, by excision, but by growth, by development from the inmost core. The process has rather been that of condensation, of sloughing off the skin, while the nucleus has been retained, in greater purity, vitality and power. " A modern theology," truly writes Dr. Forsyth, " must be an appreciation of the old, done lovingly and sympathetically, and with scientific continuity. The great authors of these systems loved and trusted at least as deeply as we do, who never have the word love off our lips— at least *as* deeply, and, on the whole, perhaps more deeply. They had among them some of the spiritual giants of the race. They thought in an atmosphere of Christian experience. Their theology was like the wounds of Christ, graven on their hearts and on the palms of their hands. To denounce and ridicule here is sheer heartlessness. The need of the hour in respect of past theologies is informed and sympathetic re-interpretation." *

THE "NEW THEOLOGY" OF TO-DAY.

The " New Theology" is the theme occupying large present attention. Its advocates and disciples are exceedingly in evidence. It declares that the old theology misinterpreted and discredited Christianity, and that its interpretation is in harmony with the changes necessitated by science and the advance of modern thought. Its claim, of course, is to give more correct expression to, and to conserve more efficiently the old faith, the pure gospel.

* " Positive Preaching and Modern Mind," p. 137.

Let us see on what grounds it makes this claim, and whether or not it effects it.

First, it emphasizes the *Immanence* of God. As one of these writers states it: "Another characteristic of to-day's thought is the certainty that God's presence is in the affairs of men. The theology of some generations ago made God an absentee Deity. He is sitting on the throne of the universe directing all things for the good of man and His own glory." Or as Dr. Dresser, in the "Philosophy of the Spirit," puts it, "He is the immanent Spirit inhabiting all the universe to its ultimate particles." He does not admit that this conception is identical with pantheism, but holds it rather to be an intermediate between the old-time deism and modern pantheism.

In regard to this arraignment of the Old Theology, we would like to know when it taught an "absentee Deity," or when it denied the immanence of God in His creation? Citations would here be in place. But as no Christian writer and no system of orthodox theology has ever made such a statement, the charge falls to the ground. The Old Testament taught that God was upon His throne ruling all His creation, but it also taught His Omnipresence in spirit and space: "If I ascend up into heaven, Thou art there; if I make my bed in hell, behold, Thou art there."* The New Testament teaches that God is "all and in all," "upholding all things by the word of His power." † And in the Church's doctrine of the Holy Spirit it has specialized this all-filling, ever-brooding presence of Deity.

The New Theology cannot insist more positively upon the immanence of Deity than did the Old, and it lays so little stress upon God's transcendence as seriously to imperil His personality. The Old Theology was only cautious not to identify God with those impersonal forces and principles which were the secondary causes by which He wrought. The New Theology does not, therefore, forefend the Old Faith as does the historic theology.

MIRACLES, THE VIRGIN BIRTH.

The Old Theology, again, holds to the supernatural agency of God, and believes in the *miracles* of the Bible, the New relegates the supernatural to the sphere of superstition. But, as Christ professed to work miracles; as the apostles did not doubt that He wrought them; as they are interwoven with the

* Ps. cxxxix. 8. † Heb. i. 3.

very fiber of the Gospels; as the fathers in this primitive period constantly refer to them with unquestioning assent; and as the Church in all times has been unwavering in her conviction of their reality, it is most difficult to see how the Old Faith is buttressed by charging that Christ deceived all witnesses by professing to heal the blind and raise the dead, when He was only using some form of hypnotism, mental suggestion, appeal to sub-conscious mind, etc.

The historic theology is built upon the true *Divinity* of Jesus Christ. It denies a human paternity and teaches the supernatural conception through the Virgin Mary. It holds Christ to be the Son of God, in the unique sense that He was pre-existent and co-substantial with the Father. The New Theology holds, with Harnack, that the "specific conception of Jesus as the Son of God does not belong to the Gospel" at all, but has been foisted upon it, so that even the liberal theologian, Loisy, makes answer: "It is his own religion, not that of the Gospel, which Harnack expounds, when he announces that "God and the soul and its God, are the whole content of the Gospel." * Christ's

* "The Gospel and the Church," p. 106.

own testimony to Peter was, that the confession of His divinity is "the Rock upon which He has built His Church," * and experience shows that upon this Rock all the forces of unbelief have spent themselves in vain.

A few years ago, when a combined effort was made by the new theologians in Germany to eliminate the Virgin Birth from the creed, as necessitating the Divine Paternity of Christ, the utter failure of the attempt shows how hopeless will be Rev. R. Campbell's scheme of establishing a Church upon a Christ from whom has been eliminated the attribute of Divinity. Speaking of the need of placing special emphasis upon this central article of the Old Theology, Dr. Henry Van Dyke says: "To imagine that we can adapt our preaching to this age of doubt by weakening, conceding, or abandoning the truth of the Deity of Christ, is to mistake the great need of our times. It is to seek to commend our Gospel by taking away from it the chief thing that men really want—an assurance of sympathy and kinship with God." †

Take from Christ His true and real divinity, and Christianity loses that sanction of authority as the

* Matt. xvi. 18.   † "Source of Authority in Religion," chap. v.

herald of absolute truth in and through which alone it holds its unique supremacy over mankind.

CHRISTIANITY A UNIQUE RELIGION.

The Old Theology taught that Judaism and Christianity were *unique*, that they constitute the self-revelation of the living God. Hence, that Christianity was not a man-made, but a God-given religion. That it was not a product of the human brain, a philosophic answer in response to the cries of man's soul, but that it was a revelation in which God spoke to men, and the record of which is given in His holy Word. The New Theology is voiced by Prof. Otto Pfleiderer, in " Early Conceptions of Christ," thus :

" As we survey the numerous points of likeness between the faith of the early Christians and the religious ideas current in the world around them, we can scarcely fail to be convinced that Christianity could not have fallen from heaven as something quite new and unique, but that it sprang up in the world of those days as the ripe fruit of ages of development and in a soil that was already prepared. Now it is, of course, easily comprehensible that this new evolutionist method of inquiry should have such a disturbing influence upon many persons, conservatives as well as critics; that they at once draw the most radical conclusions and imagine that Christianity is robbed of its unique character and its abiding worth, because it appears to be nothing more than a combination of ideas that had existed for ages, and are nowadays altogether antiquated. But such conclusions are most hasty and rash."

Another leading representative of this school, Prof. John Watson, in "The Philosophical Basis of Religion," argues that the theology of the future must take the form of a pure philosophy of religion. He claims that all attempts to base religion on revelation, or any specific divine authority, fail to satisfy the modern mind. We must either abandon all systematic thought in this field, or rebuild our theological beliefs on the basis of reason.

EVOLUTIONARY THEORY OF RELIGION.

According to this view, there were no theophanies in the Old Testament, the history of Israel was a wholly natural one, the Bible was the mere naturalistic production of a semi-barbarous age, that by a strange anomaly chanced to be the most remarkably gifted for religion in all history. And Christianity, by the science of Comparative Religion, merely takes its place as the last factor in the course of an evolution.

But the Old Faith reads the Bible as the Word of God inspired by the Holy Ghost, and recognizes Christianity as the one true religion, which must be pushed onward to the displacement and overthrow of every other. It sees the finger of God in the founding and whole course of revealed religion, and from this confidence in a divine sanction draws that missionary enthusiasm which alone can Christianize the world.

The New Theology, also, makes much of "The *Fatherhood of God*, the Brotherhood of Man, the Social and Ethical Teaching of Jesus and the Prophets." But it is impossible that it can emphasize this doctrine more than orthodox Christianity has ever done. To profess that this is a modern discovery savors of the absurd. On the contrary, that God was a Father of such passing tenderness as to give His only begotten Son, and that Christ, in dying for all, gave His followers a most vivid lesson of universal brotherhood, has been the precious inheritance of all Christian periods.

The brotherhood of man is graven on the very forefront of historical Christianity.

MODERN VIEW OF THE ATONEMENT.

Again, the new theology denies the *sacrificial* character of the death of Christ. It considers the value of His death as merely that of an example. But evangelical Christianity has ever regarded this a central doctrine. It holds that the chief significance of the death of Christ lay in its atoning power. That Christ was there giving "His life a ransom for many." That He "bare in His own body our sins upon the tree." That, having by a true incarnation, identified Himself with our humanity, He accepted the burden of the world's sin, and, acting as our representative, made a full and perfect offering in our stead, to the righteous Judge.

This doctrine, so unspeakably precious to the Christian heart, and charged with such power to draw men in loving gratitude and wonder to the foot of the cross, and forming the very substance of the Old Faith, the New Theology asks to be surrendered.

The new theology claims to exalt the *love* of God more than did the old. Hence, less emphasis is laid upon His justice, there is a less vivid recognition of *sin*, which is regarded more as an inevitable evil, in fact, a necessary stage in the process of man's evolution, and so there is less stress placed on God's judgment against it, and life is taken less seriously. As far as it is true that human progress has attained less austere views of life, and that Puritanical ideas of piety have been largely relaxed, as well as in the escape from arbitrary conceptions of divine sovereignty, there has been an undoubted gain, but this beneficent progress was made by the Church and her theology long before the appearance of the New.

For the rest, it is extremely doubtful whether, in an age of such laxity regarding sin, such disregard for the Church and the Lord's Day, such prevalence of vice, scandals in society, and corruption in business and official place, it is right or wise to gloss over the fact that God is a God of conscience as well as of love, a God who "is of purer eyes than to behold iniquity," and who "hath appointed a day" "in which He will judge the secrets of men by Jesus Christ." * On the contrary, it is one of the first duties of a real religion both to plead the love

* Rom ii. 16.

and as well to remind of that justice to which the deity is bound by the necessity of His moral nature.

LEGITIMATE SPHERES OF FAITH AND REASON.

The New Theology places *reason* above faith. It is far more religious to be rational and scientific than to be believing. The Church's historic theology holds, with Coleridge, that faith is a more primary, basal faculty than reason, and that the truths apprehended by it are higher than those cognized by the discursive reason, and are the real certainties. The philosopher, Locke, defined the relations between faith and reason, as applied to the eternal verities of religion, thus truly: " In reasonings concerning eternity, or any other infinite, we are apt to blunder and involve ourselves in manifest absurdities. But since God, in giving us the light of reason, has not thereby tied up His own hands from affording us when He thinks fit, the light of revelation in any of those matters, revelation, where God has been pleased to give it, must carry it against the probable conjectures of reason." * Faith must, indeed, be rational, but reason cannot supplant it in its legitimate sphere. Ro-

* " Essay on the Human Understanding," Book II.

manes, in his final conversion to faith, makes the confession "that he had been trying to solve this great problem of religion with only one of his faculties, that of reason, and had left out of account the testimonies of those deeper faculties which belong to the moral and spiritual nature of man."

The Old Theology has no need, then, to regret its stand for the rights and supremacy of faith. To rationalize religion is to reduce it to the narrow level of ethics, bereft of its celestial insight. Reason and science have their scope in the region of nature; to faith belongs the higher realm of the spiritual, the supernatural, the invisible and eternal. As reason is supreme in natural things, so must faith hold the scepter in the world of religion.

Similarly, the New Theology urges the pre-eminence of *life* over faith. The Gospel, it says, is a thing to be lived, not to be believed. Its teaching runs: "Attend to your life, and your faith is a matter of indifference."

The Church has ever taught that life is the outcome of faith, and that, to lead a right life, one must have the true evangelical faith. It holds that false teaching will lead the soul into dangerous paths, and hence is zealous for the pure doctrine, and deems it a duty to exclude heretics from the pulpit.

And surely here the current tenets of Christendom reflect the precepts of the Gospel. Jesus made knowledge, life and salvation dependent on faith. Paul and the great religious teachers all followed on this same line. Augustine, failing with philosophy, saved the collapsing structure of ancient civilization by the faith of the Gospel. It is the Church's confession of the pure faith, and the pulpit's preaching of the cardinal truths of the Gospel, in which to-day, as ever, lie her power to regenerate the lives and mold the conduct of men.

MYSTERY IN RELIGION RATIONAL.

The Old Faith teaches that there are *mysteries* in religion. The New Theology will have none of them. Everything must be explained, or it cannot be believed. But this will not stand the test of reason. We may not understand how God can develop from one seed a tiny blade of grass, and from another, which, under the microscope, seems identical, the mighty oak, but we can believe it. When God speaks, must we not expect to be told that which in itself may be incomprehensible?

Says Lessing: "Of what use would be a revelation that would reveal nothing?" Dr. Charles H. Parkhurst lately declared: "I revel in the mysteries of our holy faith,—the more and the greater, the surer I am that our religion is divine." Reason is, indeed, baffled at mysteries, and an un-Christian reason may recoil from them, but faith sees in these holy wonders the shining robe of Deity and adores. Truly wrote Pascal: "The last discovery of reason is that there is an infinity of things beyond reason." And again, most truly said that acute thinker: "If we submit everything to reason, our religion will have nothing in it new, divine or supernatural."

CHAPTER XXVIII.

THE OLD FAITH AND THE "NEW THEOLOGY." —CONTINUED. BACK TO CHRIST—CHRISTIAN DOGMA.

A BATTLE-CRY of the New Theology is "*Back to Christ.*" Thus Prof. Otto Pfleiderer tells us in one of his latest volumes, that he has tried by separating later accretions and by falling back upon the oldest historic sources, to approach as nearly as possible to the historic truth concerning Christ, "and to present His form, in its simple human grandeur and stripped of all mythical accessories, as the ideal of a lofty and noble religious hero, worthy of the veneration of the mind and heart of the modern world."

But a more auto-destructive slogan could not be employed. Thankfully the Church accepts the challenge. To go "back to Christ," we must go to two primary sources, the New Testament and our writers of the Post-Apostolic Age. And they afford not a particle of evidence for this merely human, white marble Christ, "this noble religious hero." But they place Him on the pedestal of Divinity, " above every name that can be named," " to which every knee should bow," whom even " the angels of God worship," and to whom all powers and principalities raise the ascription : " Thy throne, O God, is forever and ever." *

The Church to-day, as in all preceding periods, takes its stand neither on the spirit of the age, nor on the Christian consciousness, nor on the Christian principle, but on the historic and whole New Testament Christ.

The Old Theology had doctrines, had a definite faith, taught a system of beliefs—in other words, held to certain *dogmas*. On the other hand, nothing is more repellent to what assumes to be the New Theology than church dogmas. It magnifies the " faith that believes," but depreciates " the faith that is believed." It urges men to believe, but forbids them from arriving at any definite beliefs. To believe is the essence of Christianity, but to believe *something* and to be able to state it intelligently, and to hold to it loyally, it calls the essence of bigotry.

Now Paul " knew in whom he believed," and

* Heb. i. 8.

he knew *what* he believed, and he fearlessly affirmed that Christianity had certain cardinal doctrines, and of these he declared it the duty of Christians to "hold fast the form of sound words, which thou hast heard of me, in faith and love which is in Christ Jesus."* But the New Theology never fails to make Christian dogma synonymous with narrowness, intolerance and ecclesiastical tyranny.

According to it, all that the experience of Christians has attained, all that the great Christian exegetes have elicited from the study of Christ and the Gospel, all that profound Christian theologians, reflecting upon the teachings of Scripture, have formulated into simple and intelligent conceptions, is to be rejected as narrowing, hurtful and retrogressive.

NECESSITY OF DOGMA.

Nothing more than these assertions forms the staple of the New Theology, and the grounds upon which it seeks for popularity by meeting half way the secular spirit of the time. Yet no position can be more illogical and indefensible.

If anyone believes, he must believe *something*,

* 2 Tim. i. 13.

and be able to give coherent voice to it, or expect his belief to be rejected as lacking substance and reason.

A religion that exalts faith, but refuses to go before the world with a coherent, rational statement of the doctrines to which it holds, and to which it seeks to convert others, is doomed to failure, and deserves to fail. "Our spiritual possession," writes Luthardt, "subsists in no other form than that of cohering conceptions. In their common experience Christians discovered the highest and most precious content of history and of their souls. There follows, of inward necessity, an endeavor to transform these many views and feelings into a short, concise system. The experienced religion had to be intellectually formulated, and this need became imperative as wild and confused conceptions were entertained. So arose church doctrine, dogma or dogmas, in the course of a long history, so it grew to one of the mightiest forces in the life of mankind. Dogma is a historical necessity. Through it there presses into Christendom a vast, ancient treasure of Christian thoughts and conceptions of Christian sentiments and formulæ. The primary question for the Christian is not concerned

THE OLD FAITH AND THE "NEW THEOLOGY." 273

with the scientific formulæ of the dogmas, but with their quite practical aspects. But these practical things [catechism, hymn book, liturgy, devotional literature, etc.,] have received their stamp under the influence and in virtue of the power of the dogmas." *

Such is the challenge which the New Theology presents to the Church's historic theology. It is a reflex of the spirit of the time. " Those great modern traits," which Professor Woodberry specifies as "the free exercise of reason, the appeal to nature, the restless curiosity, the plea for toleration, the disposition to examine all things anew, and bring them to the test of practical reality, to think out the world afresh,"† are now, with a rash license, exercised upon the Church and her faith.

We hear the phrase, "New Thought versus Canned Theology." It is said that: "Everything has progressed except Christianity. Many thinking and progressive young men and women have been driven from the Church by the stupidity of the preachers. The pulpit is out of touch with the times, treading always the same old paths of

* "Fundamental Truths of the Christian Religion," p. 124.
† "Great Writers," p. 177.

a thousand years, hidebound and restricted in their actions, and have become the laughing stock parrots of dead Church cries instead of preachers of the living Christ."

MODERNISM.

Ever, but especially in such an aggressive, searching age, must Christianity be progressive. It must have an open mind for things that are new. So far as the New Theology is able to present new facts, to be dedicated, not as a matter of feeling, but as a matter of evidence, and in accordance with principles of a thorough scholarship, in so far the doors of the Church are wide open. Neither the Scriptures, nor Christian doctrine, nor orthodoxy itself, can maintain itself in strength and honesty, if it begins to close its eye to the actual facts. The truth is above all, and even those who have most confidence in it as it is in Christ Jesus, and as it is taught in the creeds, should have enough confidence in its ultimate ability to endure any test, to give fairest opportunity, in the proper place, for the presentation of any facts that seem to bear against it.

The attitude of the Roman Church in its antagonism to "modernism,"—resolved to cling to dogmas opposed to enlightened faith and reason, opposing religious toleration, pleading the "*semper idem*," which can only pertain to revealed truth, divorcing religion from legitimate science, and excommunicating original investigators and independent thinkers from the Church, is an extreme which confounds religion with superstition, and would oppose ignorance and bigotry to the quickening breath of modern progress.

But we must equally beware of the opposite extreme. The apostles were opposed by the reason and worldly wisdom of their age, to which the preaching of the cross was foolishness, and the fathers of our primitive age found themselves the subject of the ridicule of environing Pagan culture, but they did not yield to the temptation of dechristianizing their message that it might win the approval of the spirit of the time. On the contrary, the more bitterly the age protested against a doctrine, the more uncompromisingly they insisted on it.

THE NEW THEOLOGY OPPOSED TO THEOLOGY.

The pertinent question now is, *Does this New Theology conserve and strengthen the Old Faith?* Calling itself a Christian Theology, it was bound to proclaim this as its purpose. And very loud has been its claim that it was going to give a new and more impressive and illuminative setting to the cardinal Christian truths. It was to set the Bible on a higher pedestal of influence. It was to honor and make forceful Christianity in contrast to the Old Theology, which was discrediting and impairing it.

But does not candor compel the statement that, after a careful examination of its propositions, a theology which denies the essential Divinity of Christ, rejects the inspiration of the Scriptures, repudiates a real atonement, disbelieves the Christian mysteries, — and, accordingly, disconnects grace from the appointed means,—excludes every supernatural factor in the history of revelation, subjects faith to reason and makes life independent of belief, instead of conserving, is absolutely destructive of the old faith, and thus becomes not a true but a pseudo-theology? In fact, this New Theology is opposed to theology. It professes to believe in religion, and to hold theology as hostile to it. And this quite naturally. Theology is the philosophical or scientific statement of Christianity, its purpose being to erect bulwarks about Christianity, to make it impregnable against assault. Hence, nothing is more obnoxious to the enemies of Christianity than a systematic Christian theology. Thus Professor Zueblin, in his book, the "Religion of a Democrat," says: "Readjustment in religion is becoming a necessity. Theology is ceasing from the world and must die. Religion, then, will become more spontaneous, more genuine, more personal, and, at the same time, more social."

That this depreciation of theology should come from professedly Christian scholars and thinkers, and that it should even come from liberal theological schools themselves, is one of the anomalies of the time. Even the Unitarian thinker, James Freeman Clarke, pays this just tribute to the power of theology: "To those who think that theology is empty speculation, no longer influencing men, a study of the life and work of Augustine may teach a different lesson. Carthage, conquered and destroyed by Rome, reconquered and governed the world for fifteen hundred years through this great Christian thinker. Immense good or evil comes from the view of God, of Christ, of man, taken by Christian teachers. Theology is the body of which faith is the soul. We must have theology.

The great and deep-rooted system of Augustine will be fulfilled in something still deeper, higher, nobler and purer." *

But the New Theology, rejecting the facts and doctrines of Christianity, has nothing positive with which to construct a theology. As a building cannot be erected without wood or stone, so no theology can be framed where there are no inspired, objective, authoritative truths. As, too, it is so extremely radical, it is revolutionary, and its prevalence, so far from strengthening Christianity, would necessarily work its overthrow.

THE NEW THEOLOGY AND A NEW CHURCH.

It is altogether consistent, therefore, that Rev. R. J. Campbell, one of its most thorough-going leaders, declares that he and his adherents are finding themselves so uncomfortable and in such an inconsistent position in the orthodox churches that they must organize an independent church, based on a non-divine Christ.

Mr. Campbell is practically compelled to this step by the publication of the new Trinitarian creed, prepared and signed by the most influential leaders of English Congregationalism. The creed

* "Events and Epochs of Church History," p. 142.

was plainly an invitation to the City Temple pastor to take himself out of the Congregational fellowship, and he has no choice but to accede, since no Congregationalist of prominence stands with him. He writes: " Hitherto I have declined to take any steps in the direction of organizing the new theology movement for fear of doing anything divisive or antagonistic to the churches, but the time has come when that consideration no longer holds good."

That is, the New Theology, so far from being a necessity to give such a statement of the historic faith of Christianity as to adapt it to the present time, finds itself by an inherent necessity compelled to seek a totally new faith. Whatever its present creed be, it is forced to confess that there are retained in it so few shreds of the faith of the Gospels of the primitive period, and of the Christian beliefs of every age, that it is necessary to construct an entirely new confession.

How sweeping and destructive these claims are we learn from such an utterance as that of the German theological critic, Professor Bousset: " History would appear to destroy the idea of inspiration, that is to say, of any special revelation, in the Old and

New Testaments; the conception of redemption; the dogma of the divinity of Christ; the doctrine of the Trinity; the idea of vicarious sacrifice; the belief in the miraculous; the old view of revelation. We see how all these have been swept away in the stream of human development."

It is to be remarked that the skepticism of these writers as to the old is more than made up by their credulity as to the new.

FAILURE OF A NEGATIVE CREED.

But a creed cannot be made up of negations, and as the principle of the New Theology we thus see to be chiefly negative, the difficulty before it is a trying one.

That such a movement means inevitable failure is the teaching of history. At the height of the rationalistic movement of the eighteenth century in Germany, Bahrdt bewailed the fact that the churches where its most brilliant advocates ministered were deserted by the people, whereas, if any pastor would frequently speak of the divine Jesus, and plead the merits of the cross, the people would rally to hear him. Kuenen, the great representative of the movement in Europe, has lately complained that "if it becomes known that a candidate has studied theology at one of the radical seminaries no congregation will call him." It was a prophetic utterance of Horace Bushnell that any religious movement which wrote the word "liberalism" on its banner was doomed to certain failure, and that no such cause could progress unless it at least used the altar-terms of orthodoxy.

This simply shows that the Christian common sense correctly interprets the situation. It is convinced that Christianity is based on a revelation of vital and eternal truths, undiscoverable by reason, and giving unspeakable light and blessing to the soul. It believes that a true Christian theology should expound, illumine and defend these fundamental saving truths. And when it discovers that the so-called New Theology evades, impairs or denies the distinctive and essential doctrines of the old faith of the Gospel, verified by the common Christian experience, it is assured that it is not its friend but its enemy, and it will have none of it. It says "the old is better." Its verdict is that even of the liberal, Amiel: " I heard this morning a sermon, good, but insufficient. Why was I not edified? Because Christianity from a rationalistic point of view is a Christianity of dignity not of humility. Holiness and mysticism evaporate; the specifically Christian accent is wanting. My impression is always the same; faith is made a dull, poor thing by these attempts in the pulpit or elsewhere to reduce it to a simple moral psychology. The simple folk will say, 'They have taken away my Lord, and I know not where they have laid Him,' and they have a right to say it, and I repeat it with them." *

And even the liberal Dr. Lyman Abbott, in his late baccalaurate at Dartmouth College, finds it necessary to warn his radical collaborators: "I am a believer in the New Theology, yet I believe that any theology that scoffs at the past, any theology that commits to the waste basket all the sacred doctrines and beliefs of the ages, is a false theology. You are not to throw away the theology of the past. Sift and find the truth and apply it to present needs. We need reform, social, scientific, medical, theological reform, but the roots must be in the past."

Were the so-called liberals, and even Dr. Abbott himself, always or frequently as temperate and

* "Journal Intimé," p. 78.

judicious as this, their cause would be the stronger.

But it is just in the fact that the New Theology has detached its roots from the Christian past, and calls for a radical reconstruction of the Old Faith, in which its elemental doctrines disappear, that lie its unscripturalness, its illogicalness, its fictitious claim to be a true theology of the age, and its doom to inevitable failure.

CHAPTER XXIX.

THE CESSATION OF MIRACLES, AND MODERN HEALING CLAIMS.

It falls in with the negative tendency of the time to depreciate the value and to contest the reality of the Scriptural miracles. Thus Canon Westcott writes: "In nothing has the change of feeling during the century been more violent than in the popular estimation of miracles. At the beginning they were singled out as the masterproof of the Christian faith; now they are kept back as difficulties in the way of its reception." The Canon should have added, however, that this feeling was confined to those of rationalistic views.

The evidential value of the miracle to the minds of men is as great as ever, and the miracle can never be displaced from its integral position in the scheme of revelation. Miracles are necessary to the introduction of a new epoch in the kingdom of God. Consequently, we do not find them of continuous occurrence. But they are sent to inaugurate the epoch, and when that is sufficiently authenticated, they are withdrawn. The supernatural is only employed for the extraordinary; the necessity disappearing, the natural order resumes sway.

Accordingly, the two greatest cycles in the history of the kingdom of God, the leading forth of the Israelites to begin the history of a divine revelation, and the founding of Christianity, were the periods of the most wonderful breaking forth of miracles. Our Lord should be a competent judge. And when He said, "If I had not done among them the works which none other man did, they had not had sin,"* He taught the indisputable value of the miracle as a supreme and decisive testimony to the divinity of His mission. Miracles are demonstrative proof of the presence and power of God, and leave no excuse for unbelief. No honest reader of the New Testament can doubt that Christ professed to work miracles and meant His followers to understand that He did. Professor Seeley thus writes: "The fact that Christ appeared as a worker of miracles is the best attested fact in His whole biography." This power He also communicated to His apostles and to the seventy whom He sent forth. Without such a signal proof of divine sanction our

* John xv. 24.

Lord well knew that it would be absolutely impossible to get the ears of men in introducing a religion so totally foreign to human ideas. And that the evidential value of these initial miracles might continue for all time they were set down in the Gospel record, as John tell us: " These [signs] are written, that ye might believe that Jesus is the Christ, the Son of God, and that believing ye might have life through His name." *

MIRACLES AT EXCEPTIONAL EPOCHS.

But miracles would cease to be such if they were made a regular and ordinary mode. And if they were to break forth, occasionally, here and there, endless opportunity would be afforded for fraud, and Christian history would be thrown into disorder and utter confusion. Hence, miracles ceased at a very definite time. The apostolic period over, Christianity being sufficiently authenticated, its propagation is thenceforth to be without this visible supernatural intervention.

Consequently, there are no miracles in this Post-Apostolic Age. The great spiritual leaders who have bequeathed to us this literature neither assumed to work them nor make record of any such.

* John xx. 31.

Gibbon's testimony may be supposed to make a specific contradiction of this. He says: "The Christian Church, from the time of the apostles and their first disciples, has claimed an uninterrupted succession of supernatural gifts and miraculous powers, the gift of tongues, of vision and of prophecy, the power of expelling demons, of healing the sick and of raising the dead. The primitive Christians perpetually trod on mystic ground, and their minds were exercised by the habit of believing the most extraordinary events. The most curious or the most credulous among the Pagans were often persuaded to enter into a society which asserted an actual claim of miraculous powers." *

Gibbon is here led into error by his cynical skepticism toward Christianity, and by his desire to give a discreditable reason for its remarkable growth. In reply, Dr. Middleton wrote: "From the time of the apostles there is not a single instance of this miracle [raising the dead] to be found in the first three centuries. And Chrysostom [fourth century], in a remarkable passage, affirms the long discontinuance of miracles to be a notorious fact." It

* "Decline and Fall of the Roman Empire," Vol. I., chap. xv.

is one thing to make assertions and another to write genuine history.

The remarkable passage to which Middleton refers occurs in a very temperate and judicious discussion by Chrysostom of the special and limited purpose of the miracle, and in a discriminating argument against the attempt of fanatics to use it in behalf of their propaganda. Chrysostom first rejects the miracles of Christ's infancy: "Hence, it seems clear to us that the miracles which they say belong to Christ's childhood are false and the inventions of those who bring them into notice. For, if He had begun at His early age to work wonders, how could John have been ignorant of them?"[*]

Here follows the passage: "Miracles were wrought also in the Old Testament among the Jews when wandering in the wilderness; as also in our case; for among us, too, when we had just come out of error, many wonderful works were shown forth, *but afterwards they stayed*, when in all countries true religion had taken root."[†]

So we find no account of even supernatural signs in this sub-apostolic time. Even the gift of tongues

[*] Homily XVII. on St. John.
[†] Gospel of St. Matthew, Homily IV.

THE CESSATION OF MIRACLES. 289

has wholly ceased. And to this assertion the visions of Hermas form no exception, for they are confessedly clothed throughout in the imagery of symbolism. Nor is there anything supernatural in the account of the vision of Ignatius after his martyrdom. It is merely a vision in a dream, as is evident: "Having slept the whole night in tears, and having entreated the Lord with much prayer, it came to pass on our falling into a brief slumber, that some of us saw the blessed Ignatius suddenly standing by and embracing us." *

Miracles, then, of all kinds had ceased in the sub-apostolic age. Imitation of them was regarded as the attempt to employ evil, occult powers, and was thus repudiated by Ignatius: "When Christ was manifested to the world every kind of magic was destroyed, and every bond of wickedness disappeared, and the kingdom of evil was abolished." †

NO CLAIM OF MIRACLES.

There is, in fact, a remarkable absence of miraculous signs, such as we might think it perfectly natural would yet have lingered in this age, even as the rays of the sun illumine the horizon after he has

* "Martyrdom of Ignatius," chap. vii.
† Epistle to the Ephesians, chap. xix.

set from view. And that, in their extreme needs and dangers, no assertion of extraordinary powers or confirming signs was made, shows both the poise and sanity of these leaders, and also that a clear line of demarcation was drawn between this and the apostolic period. Nothing could be more convincing to prove that one of the clearest of these marks was the cessation of the miracle.

This conclusion is fully borne out by the learned Bishop Lightfoot, who calls attention to the absence of miraculous events in the patristic writings. Speaking of the epistle of the Smyrnaeans, describing the martyrdom of Polycarp, in which some marvelous signs are reported by the witnesses, he says: "Considering all the circumstances of the case, we have more occasion to be surprised at the comparative absence than at the special prominence of the supernatural in the narrative. Compared with records of early Christian martyrs, or with biographies of mediæval saints, or with notices of religious heroes at any great crisis, even in the more recent history of the Church, as, for instance, the rise of Jesuitism, or of Wesleyanism, this document contains nothing which ought to excite a suspicion." *

* "Apostolic Fathers," Vol. I., p. 614.

The assertion, therefore, of the Christian Scientists that Christ meant the gift of supernatural power to belong to His followers for all time is disproved. So the advocacy of the healing ministry of the Church, as lately made, on the ground that the practice is merely a return to observances of the early Church, involves a total misreading of history. The *Christian Register* is correct in saying: " For the clergy to ignore the verdict of the ages and attempt to revive an outgrown function will be harmful to both public health and to the Christian Church as it would be for surgeons to substitute magic for anæsthetics, or for doctors to give physic when repentance of sin is needed."

MODERN HEALING CLAIMS.

Two points are especially worthy of note in the modern claim for healing in the Church, as put forth by the Emmanuel Movement of Dr. Worcester. The first is, that the statement that it is a return to the practice of the early Church is altogether equivocal. If it refers to what will be generally understood as the early Church—that immediately succeeding Christ and the apostles—it is absolutely untrue. If it refers to a later period, entirely dissevered from the origin of Christianity, and arising from a perversion of it, then such a corrupted origin utterly invalidates its authority. Or, if it refers to Christ and the apostles, then it is a groundless appeal, for no later period can lay claim to their extraordinary and supernatural powers.

"The point I want you to understand," says the Rev. Hugh Birckhead, rector of St. George's Episcopal Church, New York, "is that the miracles which Christ regarded as important evidential proof of His power have never stopped." The proof adduced for this is that given by the Christian Scientists, viz., Christ's assertion to His apostles: "And greater works than these shall he do." * But that these words were not to be taken literally is manifest from the impossibility of doing greater miracles of nature than Christ did. Hence the Church has universally interpreted the words in a spiritual sense, referring to the miracles to be wrought by the Holy Spirit in the soul's re-birth and re-creation. So Luther : "These great spiritual miracles happen every day, viz., in that Christ's word produces faith, gives blessedness and peace." But no one more decisively than Luther denounced

* John xiv. 12.

the miraculous claims of the Zwickau prophets as false and fanatical pretense.

The second point is suggested by Dr. Worcester's book, in which, while claiming extraordinary gifts of healing for the Church to-day, he rejects the miracles of Christ as either simple instances of hypnotism or mental therapeutics. True miracles, the mighty works, which Christ claimed to work, Dr. Worcester does not believe He really could do. It is characteristic of religious charlatanry that while it exalts its own artifices and powers, it should depreciate the omnipotent working of the Master.

The Emmanuel movement is based upon such a fusion of mind and body as to make its philosophy or psychology a species of materialistic monism. It rests upon the same basis as that of Dubois, a leading authority on psychotherapy—mental healing—whose position is frankly that of materialistic monism. This is a repudiation of the foundation of Christianity.

Accordingly, while he glorifies Christian Science, saying: " I venture to say that the rise of Christian Science is the most significant phenomenon that has taken place in our generation," he characterizes the Church as dying: " This is new life for the Church, for the lack of which the Church is dying."

But the Church is still alive and powerful as the organism for man's spiritual life, and will wisely turn a deaf ear to the "clerical clinic" that would first diagnose her as in a dying state, and then seek to revive her by a false union of religion and pseudo-science.

The Church was commissioned not to heal the bodies but the souls of men. The credentials of her divine authority are not to be confounded with her spiritual purpose. The miracles necessary to validate it merely took the form of healing that the divine power might be exercised beneficently. That feature was wholly incidental and secondary. Accordingly it passed with its occasion.

DANGER OF PERVERSION OF THE CHURCH.

The great purpose of the Church is no modern discovery. Through all the ages it has witnessed of the invisible things of God and ministered to man's spiritual being and called him to his eternal welfare. When drawn aside from this high mission, or when commingling it with non-religious schemes and efforts, the Church is dangerously compromised and suffers incalculable loss of power.

Physical miracles have ceased, and she can no longer lay claim to their exercise, but the spiritual miracle of the regeneration of the soul and the growing sanctification of the spirit into the divine image, belongs to her perpetual agency, and history continually adds to her record wonderful and glorious examples.

The attempt to drag the Church into the medical arena and to institute an ecclesiastical department of psychotherapy is a violation of the spirit and purpose of the Church, against which primitive history and all the pure Christian eras protest. Such movements are but a politic appeal to the sensation-loving spirit of the time, and those who run after them are seriously misled as to that faith, repentance and spiritual healing, which the Church is commissioned to preach to a world lying in the bondage of sin and death. Christianity ever suffers serious hurt from temporizing with such false popular tendencies, and alone by promptly rejecting them can maintain her unique spiritual mission and the supremacy of her moral power.

CHAPTER XXX.

INFERIORITY OF THE PATRISTIC LITERATURE TO THE INSPIRED WRITINGS OF THE NEW TESTAMENT.

TISCHENDORF dates the Muratori document, which gives the first catalogue of the books of the New Testament which from the earliest period were considered canonical and sacred, at about 150 A. D. At the head of the list it places our four Gospels.

A little later, perhaps, 160 or 170, we have the Syriac version, called the Peschito, and the Latin, named Italic, showing their wide acceptance. At a still earlier date, 139 A. D., Justin Martyr, in his first apology to the emperor, makes the statement that the "memoirs of the apostles, called Gospels, were read after the prophets every Lord's Day in the assemblies of the Christians."

In the recently found "Apology of Aristides," addressed to Emperor Hadrian (about 140 A. D.), Aristides speaks of the Gospels as written, and

INFERIORITY OF THE PATRISTIC LITERATURE. 297

offers the emperor the Christian Scriptures, thus confirming what is suggested in Barnabas, and sustaining the position of Justin.

And Tatian, in his "Diatesseron" (combination of four), the earliest harmony of the Gospels, tells us that they were widely read in the churches.

These testimonies bring us close to the verge of the first century, and show that practically at the death of the Apostle John, the books of the New Testament were generally read in the churches on the same level as the books of the Old Testament, and hence regarded as inspired.

THE PATRISTIC WRITINGS READ AT PUBLIC WORSHIP.

Now, it is a fact that the writings of our post-apostolic fathers were also read for edification in the churches. Eusebius, the Church historian, who gives the account of the Council of Nice in 325, thus states "that the Epistles of Clement were publicly read for instruction in most of the churches, both in foreign times and in our own." *
And there is abundant testimony that the writings of Hermas and the other great spiritual leaders were similarly read. This, in a time of such

* "Ecclesiastical History," Vol. III., chap. xvi.

trouble and persecution, was most natural and proper. These letters sounded like a clarion call of faith and courage, to strengthen and hold together, and mutually comfort the widely scattered and sorely tried congregations.

And it is beyond question true that these epistles were held in the highest veneration, and were referred to by Irenæus, Tertullian and Origen as sacred or inspired, not using the term in the strictest sense, as it is also the fact that there was for a time considerable confusion as to whether or not some of them should not be recognized as *quasi*-Scriptural.

But, on the other hand, they were never placed on a level with the canonical gospels and epistles, for although the canon had not yet been definitely fixed, there existed in the Christian consciousness a definite conviction of the bridgeless chasm that separated an inspired from a non-inspired author. The period of a supernatural agency of the Holy Spirit necessary to produce an inspired writing was ended, and however much their great and holy teachers might be venerated, no one thought of according to them the authority attached to the utterances of Christ and His apostles.

NOT REGARDED INSPIRED.

An examination of this literature shows this to be borne out by the internal evidence. The post-apostolic fathers make not the least claim to inspiration. They preface no statement with a "Thus saith the Lord," or with "It was given me by the revelation of Jesus Christ," as do the inspired writers. Moreover, they ever cite the books of the New Testament as Scripture, deferring to their authority as absolute. They do not assume to originate, but only to comment upon the received Scriptures.

Their style, also, quite lacks the force and creative character of the writings which compose the New Testament. Canon Farrar, in defending the canonical character of the Second Epistle of Peter, comments on this fact thus : "A consideration of capital importance is the superiority of this epistle to every one of the uncanonical writings of the first and second centuries. Who will venture to assert that any apostolic father—that Clement of Rome, or Ignatius, or Polycarp, or Hermas, or Justin Martyr, could have written so much as twenty consecutive verses so eloquent and so powerful as those of the Second Epistle of St. Peter?" * The critic,

* "Early Days of Christianity," chap. viii., p. 115.

Renan, likewise calls attention to the "immense superiority and discourses of divine beauty in the Gospels." *

This is a notable fact. Some of the writers of this next generation were remarkable for ability, as, for example, the author of the Epistle to Diognetus, and evinced qualities of character and leadership of the highest type. But when we compare their writings with those of the New Testament we do not find those great original truths, those creative thoughts which give us pause, which shine by their own light, which we feel none but authors "inspired by the Holy Ghost" could have written. The difference marks the line between *Theopneustic* (God-inspired) and naturalistic writing.

Nevertheless, we must give these writers their due. Their letters or epistles or homilies are marked by the deepest devotion, by a profound spirituality, by thorough familiarity with the Old and New Testament Scriptures, and by the finest precepts of practical piety. Many passages are of great elevation, and, if they do not approach the New Testament, yet breathe a lofty religious sentiment, such as would make their reading illuminating and stimulative to the modern Christian mind.

* "Life of Jesus," chap. xxviii., p. 259.

GREAT CHARACTERS, NOT GREAT WRITERS.

"The apostolic fathers," it has been justly said, "are not great writers, but great characters." They present a marked contrast to the depth and clearness of conception with which the several apostolic writers place before us different aspects of the Gospel, and by which their title to a special inspiration is vindicated. But there is a breadth of moral sympathy, a simplicity and a fervor of Christian devotion which are the noblest testimony to the influence of the Gospel.

"The gentleness and severity of Clement, whose whole spirit is absorbed in contemplating the harmonies of nature and of grace; the fiery zeal of Ignatius, in whom the one overmastering desire of martyrdom has crushed all human passion; the unbroken constancy of Polycarp, whose protracted life is spent in maintaining the faith once delivered to the saints—these are lessons which can never become antiquated or lose their value." *

Take as an illustration the following stirring sentences from Barnabas's "The Way of Light": "Thou shalt love Him that created thee; thou shalt glorify Him that redeemed thee from death. Thou shalt not let the Word of God issue from thy

* "Apostolic Fathers," Lightfoot, Vol. I., p. 7.

lips with any kind of impurity. Thou shalt be meek; thou shalt be peaceable. Thou shalt not be mindful of evil against thy brother. Thou shalt not be joined in soul with the haughty. Receive thou as good things the trials which come upon thee. Thou shalt not issue orders with bitterness to thy maid-servant, or thy man-servant, who trust in the same God. Do not be ready to stretch forth thy hands to take, whilst thou contractest them to give. Thou shalt seek out every day the faces of the saints and meditate how to save a soul by thy word. Thou shalt not make a schism, but thou shalt pacify those that contend by bringing them together. Thou shalt confess thy sins. Thou shalt not go to prayer with an evil conscience. This is the way of light." *

* Epistle, chap. xix.

CHAPTER XXXI.

GENERAL VIEW. LESSONS FOR THE PRESENT.

As a summary of the results of this study of these Post-Apostolic Fathers, we note these dominant characteristics.

A CREATIVE EPOCH.

All these writers are permeated with the enthusiasm of a new-born time. They feel that they live in a creative epoch. There is a second beginning of things. The breath of a new morning has awakened the world. The Creator has stood upon the earth, and has said: "Behold, I make all things new."* An all-pervasive conviction animates their minds that a new spiritual force for individuals and the human race has appeared.

The first creation was material; this is the second—the moral creation. The mystery of a divine origin and potency confronts them. Thus writes Ignatius: "Now three mysteries of renown

* Rev. xxi. 5.

are wrought in silence by God. The old kingdom disappears, and God Himself is manifested in human form, for the renewal of life. In our day the divine decree has made a new beginning." * A new religion, a new type of character, a new soul-passion, a new birth of humanity is in the air. It is the first chapter of the coming golden age of mankind. It bears the potency of a new era of human rights, a new brotherhood, a reconstructed civilization.

It is the spiritual *renaissance* of history. Miracles will be wrought in the moral sphere. The Christ-spirit shall dominate the sons of men. A new ethical code shall prevail among nations. The whole social state of men shall be recast after the Christian pattern. The new heaven of love shall overarch a new earth of righteousness and peace. The world has shaken off the lethargy and despair of the ages, and sets forth upon a career of inspiration, energy and hope. The spirit of progress is rife. Forward is the word! On, on, to the fulfillment of the glorious counsels of God. A creative breath from the eternal throne has swept over all the face of the earth.

* Epistle to the Ephesians, chap. xix.

A TRUE CHRISTIAN IDEALISM.

This conviction of the divine re-creative force and purpose appearing in Christianity inspired the primitive fathers with what they constantly manifest—a noble Christian idealism. Christ had taught that His disciples should have for their aim the regeneration and reform of society and the world. This could be effected alone by sacrifice—the last effort of love. He had said their prime motive should be: "He that findeth his life shall lose it, and he that loseth his life for my sake shall find it." *

It is this aim at the evangelization of the world through the Crucified, as shown in the spirit of sacrifice, which burns in the hearts of the primitive leaders. They will supplant the Pagan spirit by a character less sensual than the Greek; less martial than the Roman; less proud than the Stoic; less bigoted than the Jew; and greater than all in the might of love, the beauty of purity, the victorious power of truth.

The conclusion which the great moralists of the past have hitherto reached is that high aims may be ridiculous; that heroism often is folly; that the

* Matt. x. 39.

finer the soul the more utter its earthly defeat. The moral ideals of the race, how sublime; but oh! the irony of it at last, and no form of it so ironical as the will to serve mankind, the passion for reforming the world!

But with this cumulative experience of humanity against them, these men abated not one jot of their high moral idealism. This is the passion that controls all their thoughts, words and deeds. Though they lose all, and give their bodies to the lions or to the flaming pyre, yet they will transform and save the world. This was the ideal which the Lord had left in visible form before their eyes, and to translate it into reality was their high and tireless resolve.

And this same Christian idealism has had its heroes since, as in a St. Bernard, a St. Boniface, a St. Francis, and in the representative Christians of every age. In a world where materialism seems to crush society in its octopus grasp, and where pessimism sinks so many brave hearts, and where the irony of justice fills many a noble spirit with despair, the Christian Church holds aloft this idealism of the triumph of righteousness, love and brotherhood.

UNIVERSALITY OF VISION.

The transforming mission to which the Post-Apostolic Fathers had committed their lives embraced nothing less than the horoscope of the world. There appeared for the first time now upon the historic stage an universal religion. As Harnack says: "It is an astonishing fact in the history of the Gospel that it left its native soil and went forth into the wide world and realized its universal character. It became a world-religion, in that, having a message for all mankind, it preached it to Greek and Barbarian." *

Judaism received its complement in Christianity. There was proclaimed but one God, and He not a tribal or national God, but "the God of all the peoples of the earth." This was a truth totally new to mankind and at cross-purposes with all the traditions and experiences of the race. It was the conception which made the primitive Church a great missionary organization and which has given birth to modern Home and Foreign Missions. Its principle was, that as God was the Father of all men, so should all men be brothers, and that there should not be an antagonism of faiths and interests, but a community of belief and of mutual welfare.

* "History of Dogma," pp. 11 and 12.

One universal Church, under the spiritual supremacy of which Christian states were to guarantee equal rights to all, was to engirdle the globe. "It was Christianity that broke down the wall of partition between ranks, nations and states. Not before did there exist on earth such a thing as international law, upon which, in our day, the whole framework of society depends. That we have liberty of conscience, that right and law form the foundation of national life, and that commerce and a general civilization of mankind have been rendered possible on earth, are blessings for which we are indebted to Christianity." *

This magnificent conception of a universal spiritual empire filled the early Christian with a sublime enthusiasm and armed him with a wand of might. But it also involved the assertion of the uniqueness of Christianity, and therefore for its realization obligated its advocates to the overthrow of all the age-long religions and the subversion of every Pagan deity to the scepter of One crucified as a malefactor.

* "The Fundamental Truths of Christianity," Lecture X., Luthardt.

THE CERTITUDE OF FAITH.

With such a seemingly utopian scheme and with such unequal odds against them, with their utter feebleness against the force of intellect and the overwhelming superiority of material power, nothing is a greater moral miracle than the absolute assurance of our Christian fathers.

Universal agnosticism confronts them, but "they know in whom they have believed." No show of force, no fire of persecution, no apparent defeat can shake the perfect security of their faith. They are so irrefutably grounded in the gospel that their confidence in all its blessed truths cannot be moved. No other explanation of this unique phenomenon can be given than that they had realized the Christian faith in a personal experience. They knew by a positive, inner testimony that "the Lord was working with them and confirming the word with signs following." *

Certainty was their one watchword as to all the cardinal doctrines and promises of the gospel. The truths of Christianity had become such living and eternal verities that nothing on earth or in hell could shake their conviction.

* Mark xvi. 20.

And this certitude, as it ever does, gave them power. To those who thus preach, the truth becomes a tangible thing, an incarnate energy. The ancient world, with its religious indifference and its philosophic doubt, could not stand before this energy of invincible confidence that animated the army of the cross. The result verified the saying of the beloved disciple: "This is the victory that overcometh the world, even our faith." * So astonishing was the progress of Christianity in the face of the most appalling obstacles that already Justin Martyr could boast: "There exists not a people, whether Greek or Barbarian, or any other race of men, whether they dwell under tents or wander about in covered wagons, among whom prayers are not offered up in the name of a crucified Jesus to the Father and Creator of all things." †

What a lesson this faith of these spiritual heroes to us whose faith is so often feeble and wavering, though we now have twenty centuries of its triumphs to confirm and strengthen it! And what a warning, also, as to those who to-day wish us to weaken in our faith all along the line as the only means to success! On the contrary, we learn here

* 1 John v. 4. † "Dialogue with Tryphon."

that it is only where Christian teachers and ministers are armed with this indubitable certitude as to the great truths of the gospel that the Church will go forth and continue to conquer as of old.

PAST AND FUTURE.

The face of Christianity in this era is towards the future. She feels that hers is a mission of conquest. The coming generations are to be hers. She is to press forward and onward to the throne of the world. And ever and ever is she to lift humanity to greater heights. Progress—spiritual and material—is to be her note. Under her sceptre sin is to be dethroned, ignorance banished, misery relieved, and liberty, intelligence and happiness to reach their highest phase. Onward, to an earth redeemed and transfigured with grace—a truly Christian era!

But while her conquering career thus lies towards the future, her inspiration must ever be drawn from the past. Only by looking backward to Christ and the apostolic times can she go forward to victory. The course of Christianity is cast amid the current of the ages. She must address herself to the needs and problems of the present. But to meet these adequately, she must renew her strength, revive her energy and reburnish her arms from that age whence she derived her origin. The present emerges from the past, and is the soil out of which must grow the future. He who discards the moral unity of the ages puts himself out of touch with the universal order. He forgets the great truth in Tennyson's couplet:

"Yet I doubt not through the ages, one increasing purpose runs,
And the thoughts of men are widened with the process of the suns."

Says Schleiermacher: "The tree of Christianity, to be flourishing and vigorous to-day, must have its roots struck deeply into the soil of the past."

So, while the outlook of this period is towards coming times, there is never a severance from the old foundations. The "fullness of the times" lies back of them, the fullness of the dominion before them. And so their message is at once old and new, is redolent of the past and adapted to the living present. It unites antiquity and modernity. It is age-long and yet breathes the spirit of the times. It pulsates with a universal life. Christianity is surely progressive, because it is wisely conservative. We never think of Christianity as a thing of yesterday or of to-morrow only. It is of both. Therefore it is an eternal force in the world. "You are an American," said a Brahman to a traveler, "and I am an Asiatic. You belong to a conquering faith; I belong to a dying faith." Every ethnic faith save Christianity is on the road to death. Not one has the power of expansion. The so-called ethnic faiths are dying faiths. But Christianity, built upon the past, spanning the current of the ages, ever presses towards the future, gaining a wider horizon and a larger career.

CHAPTER XXXII.

GENERAL VIEW—CONTINUED. AUTHORITY OF THE POST-APOSTOLIC AGE.

CHRISTIANITY, being thus an historical religion, naturally is under the influence of history. And those ages most instinct with the life and power of the gospel are most potential with it. Of all these periods, the Post-Apostolic, next to the New Testament, Augustinian and Reformation eras, is most weighty. For, if Christianity be historical, then it must have an unbroken continuity of life, reaching back to its origin. And that which is nearest its source represents its most pristine purity.

Doctrines and rites, originating subsequent to this age, lack real historical authority. For unless their roots, at least, are found here, they are not connected by the smallest link with Christ and the apostles. They are totally severed from primitive Christianity. The contiguity of the teachers of this period to the beginning, their personal touch with the apostles, and through them with Christ Himself, gave them a view of the new religion so direct, unique and all-pervasive as to be a source of authority to which every succeeding age, in some respects, must defer.

On that question, most vital and absorbing to us to-day, " What is Christianity ? " what its essential feature, what its original content, what its primitive form, who was Christ, and what were His teachings? they had such an opportunity as no succeeding age could have. Their testimony lay at first hand. They could inquire as to the meaning of every doctrine, investigate every fact, solve every inconsistency and contradiction. If they had prepossessions, they were of such recent date that they could easily have freed themselves from them. Every motive was against their acceptance of Christianity. And that, at such extreme loss and sacrifice, they accepted and held it in substantially the form in which it has overspread the world, can only be explained by their overwhelming conviction, that they had it as Christ delivered it, and that their consciences were irrevocably bound by it. There is every reason, then, to believe that the Christianity they confessed was drawn from its purest original type.

Shall it be said that these writers were ignorant

of modern science, knew nothing of evolution, were not acquainted with advanced thought, had not our wide intellectual outlook, and that therefore they lack authority for our time?

The reply is that we are here in quite another sphere. It is not with material progress or with speculative philosophies that we have to deal. But the questions are those relating to the spiritual sphere, to revelation, to faith, to Christianity, to religious insight, and to their historical setting and facts. These were within the witness of those living in the primitive age as of no other, and hence do they have an authority, of a kind, unequaled in the field of Christian history.

A FORMATIVE AGE.

Such an era must naturally have been a fruitful field of inquiry, and have afforded the most satisfactory results for all those who in succeeding times sought for side lights upon the origin of Christianity. And so Church history shows the formative character of this period in the molding of Christianity and in its gaining definitive and ordered statements.

As the Apostle John, having had a generation to

think over the teachings of Christ, saw in them deeper views of divinity than did the synoptic evangelists, so the Post-Apostolic Fathers began that process of study, reflection and assimilation which made the beginning of a scientific presentation of Christian doctrine.

To these patristic writings, in conjunction with the New Testament, the great leaders of the next century went for those ideas which they developed by degrees into a systematic Christian theology. "The Christianity of the third century," says Seeberg, " presents itself to us as a direct continuation of the doctrinal teachings of the second century. The roots of the ideas here developed may in almost every instance be traced back to the Apostolic Fathers." * As the great aim of these Fathers had been to interpret and appropriate in its purest and fullest form the saving truth transmitted by the apostles, so their teachings helped Irenæus in the first effort of a great thinker to frame a churchly theology. Likewise Tertullian only furthered their work in defining and fixing the Christology of the west. Similarly their views exerted a shaping force upon the Alexandrian theology and its great representative, Origen. So,

* " History of Doctrines," Part II., chap. i.

again, Athanasius finds here strong support for the doctrine of the Trinity; and Augustine learns of salvation through grace alone; and Anselm is here sustained in his fuller gospel view of a substitutionary atonement.

And, in the Reformation era, it is to the study of this period, as far as uninspired history was concerned, that Luther goes to purify the Church of those later innovations and corruptions against which the purity of this time was a protest. When Luther appealed to the Scriptures, and when Eck said that he could not refute him out of the Scriptures, but that he could from the Fathers, Luther was able to make answer that the Apostolic Fathers were greater authority than the Mediæval Schoolmen, and that none of the errors against which he protested were countenanced by them or existed in their time. Thus this Post-Apostolic became a formative age for the Christian theology of all succeeding periods of the Church, and from their immemorial thrones these fathers still sway the christian world.

OF LIVING AND PRESENT-DAY INTEREST.

Truth never becomes antiquated. The older it grows the more it proves its claim to live. It becomes venerable but not senile, gathering greater authority with the lapse of years. It is endued with the " power of an endless life."

So is the study of every period of christian history a study of truth in the toils of conflict and experience, and hence of living interest and instruction. Hence we find that while the writings of their classic contemporaries are known but to the scholarly few, and their themes touch the present very remotely, if at all, the questions discussed by these primitive fathers are full of vitality for our time. They are just such as are burning ones today. Their difficulties are our difficulties; the attacks they have to meet are such as meet us; the bulwarks they defend are the very ones we are guarding; the doubts against which they must contend are largely identical with those of to-day.

For example, we may well compare the utterly alien spirit of Roman skepticism and stoical contempt for the distinctive doctrines of the new Christian faith, with that boastful, and, we may say, supercilious confidence with which modern science and philosophy often assail the doctrines and supernatural claims of Christianty as being rendered impossible and relegated to outworn superstition by our enlarged knowledge.

And as their problems and difficulties and dilemmas were largely coincident with those of Christians in this age of criticism, negation and doubt, so can we learn from their conduct under similar fire.

NO COMPROMISE WITH THE AGE SPIRIT.

And we see that there was no attempt at compromising with the wisdom of this world. No effort was made to adapt these tenets of Christianity most hostile to unregenerate reason, so that they would be acceptable to current systems of thought. At a later period, Origen did attempt to unite with the Christian doctrines the profound speculations of the Gnostics, so that Christianity could maintain its standing with the literary circles of the time. But the hope that this compromise would succeed met with lamentable failure. It neither saved the Church's beliefs nor propitiated her opponents. And it caused untold harm and weakening to the cause, felt for generations after.

But our Apostolic Fathers stood out firmly against this temptation. They neither disguised nor pared down the distinctive and offensive features of Christianity. But they set forth the pure, simple and entire gospel as they had received it, whether men would hear or whether they would forbear. They were convinced that their message was of Christ and God, and that this divine authority would give them the victory.

And if thus faithful these primitive Christian heroes stood, in an ancient world of culture so directly antagonistic to their message, and if through this fidelity they triumphed, let the modern Church learn a lesson.

There can be no compromise of our faith sufficient to placate its opponents which will not surrender the fundamentals of the gospel. The only method of honesty, as well as of success, is to hold forth the pure old gospel in all its simplicity, fullness and power. We cannot bring the world into allegiance to the Church by interpreting Christianity in harmony with the wisdom of the world.

CHAPTER XXXIII.

GENERAL VIEW—CONCLUDED. ESSENTIAL IDENTITY OF PRIMITIVE AND MODERN CHRISTIANITY.

THE supreme fact which emerges from the study of the writings of the Post-Apostolic Fathers is that the conception of Christianity they set forth is, in its main features, coincident with that of orthodox Christianity to-day. The central dominant thought of the primitive fathers is that of the divinity of the Lord Jesus Christ. Ignatius, Clement, Barnabas and all, worship Christ as the eternal Son who came to reveal God, and, through His redemptive offering, to restore man to his Father.

This primitive idea of Christianity appeared as the characteristic feature in the second and third centuries. Thus says Seeberg: "A general view of the historical development thus far traced leads to the conviction that the Christianity of the Apostolic Fathers was that which characterized the Church of the second century. Everywhere we note the consciousness of the sinner's lost condition and the conviction that he can be saved only through grace, through Christ, through the sacred ordinances of the Church." *

THE CENTRAL DOGMA.

Of the succeeding Nicene Age, in which were settled those great fundamental doctrines which became regulative of the Christian faith in all succeeding times, Harnack affirms: "Athanasius brought everything back to the thought of redemption through God Himself—*i. e.*, through the God-man, who is of the *same essence* with God. He was not concerned about a formula, but about a decisive basis for faith, about redemption unto a divine life through the God-man." †

This was the central dogma somewhat confusedly held during the degeneracy of the Middle Ages. In the Reformation we see it republished in all its pristine purity and power. It was held alike by Wesley and the High Church Tractarians and the great modern preachers.

It is the backbone of every great Church confession. The history of church doctrine shows the divine, redeeming Christ as that truth which runs through Christian theology as the keel stretches

* "Text-Book of the History of Doctrine," Part I., chap. iv.
† "History of Dogma." Part IV., Book I.

the whole length of the ship, giving support to every brace and timber in it. It is that central truth in every age, in the light of which the whole Christian scheme was seen in variant forms.

THE CRADLE OF CHRISTIAN THEOLOGY.

All the proof overwhelmingly refutes the assertion that this and the dependent generic doctrines were the growth of a later age, inventions of philosophical thought, formulas devised to uphold special systems of theology.

On the contrary, not alone do we see them dominant in every period, but the closer we get back to the New Testament original, the more vital and all-controlling do we find them. Primitive, Mediæval and Modern Christianity are at one in these three essential statements: The Fall of Man; A Divine Revelation; Its Purport, Redemption through the Incarnation of Christ, the God-man. Look at Christianity in any age, in any phase, in any theology, these cardinal doctrines emerge. To this primary doctrine all variant views have been but secondary and incidental.

But now we are confronted with the challenge that after these twenty centuries of identity, there must be an essential change.

President Schurman tells us that we are on the brink of a revolution where not merely the divisive lines between the denominations will disappear, but those which differentiate Christianity itself from ethnic faiths. Another great literary writer asserts that we are "passing through the crisis of the de-christianization of the modern world."[*] And on all sides, even from ministers, commentators and theologians we hear the demand that Christianity submit to a radical readjustment of its beliefs, aligning them with the philosophical deductions of scientists, and with the rationalistic and monistic materialism of modern thought, or that it must pass from its spiritual thraldom over men.

MODERNISM.

In response, let us contrast these two conceptions. The one, as given in a recent volume, "The Programme of Modernism," asserts that there has been no revelation. That all that is supernatural in Christianity is false. That the only religion man can have he must evolve. That the only truth he can get he must discover through the exercise of his natural faculties. Hence, such a thing as truth—in the real or absolute sense—is impos-

[*] Professor Woodberry, "Makers of Literature, p. 143."

sible. Commenting sympathetically on the book, the *Outlook* says: "If Christ came to give an *unalterable dogma*, He did not come to give life, for life will as certainly demand change in the dogma which expresses it as the life of the artist will demand different artistic expression at different periods of his development. The authors of 'The Programme of Modernism' make no attempt to obscure this issue."

The significance, then, of this modern critique of Christianity is clear. There is no settled objective truth. As the human mind is fallible, so its view of truth will always be shifting, indefinite and uncertain. With Montaigne it must ever cry dubiously: "What can I know?" Upon all the questions for which the soul seeks answer with unutterable yearning, there can be no light. The quest of the ages remains a sphinx, the seekers after God are blind as in the pre-Christian eras. There is nothing upon which man can build or rest—no security, no light, no hope—nothing but the ancient classic despair, or the modern rayless agnosticism.

The physical universe has its fixity, its laws, its central unity and order. But the spiritual universe lacks reality. Truth does not sit upon the throne.

No bond of authority holds it under the sway of law. Liberty of thought is the central principle. Everyone can think as he pleases, and form what opinions he will, for there is no truth, no criterion of error, no spiritual supremacy. This system means not lawful freedom, but unlimited license of opinion, with its necessary correlatives of doubt, ignorance and spiritual darkness.

Over against this negative scheme of Modernism stands that which has ever been, and is still, the distinctive christian conception. It is that man by his natural reason cannot know God, has never thus found Him, and is just as greatly in darkness amid his modern progress as ever, as evinced, for example, by the tragic farewell words of the philosopher, Spencer. But it has pleased God to give a revelation, through His co-eternal, co-divine Son. As God is the Truth, so the revelation of Jesus Christ is true. Being the Truth, it is perfect, without error. As such it is authoritative, and fallible human reason must defer to it. Faith is the spiritual organ of its reception.

CHRISTIANITY A RELIGION OF AUTHORITY.

Christianity thus becomes a religion of Truth, and hence of authority. It proclaims the Gospel and calls upon all men to believe. Bishop Gore, in his recent volume, "The New Theology and the Old Religion," thus summarizes it: "There is an essential difference between human nature and divine nature; religious truth cannot be arrived at by the human faculties; it is furnished to men in a completed revelation; and a summary of that revelation is to be found in the Apostles' and Nicene Creeds, which are to be accepted by faith."

The Church is made the guardian of this revelation, of which the Scriptures are a reliable record. And as Truth is perfect and unchangeable, so the generic marks of the Church are identical in every age. And, while this message of revealed, flawless, unchanging truth is the chief point of opposition and attack, it is yet that which distinguishes Christianity as a God-given religion and gives it its unique power over the minds and hearts of men. Even so liberal a theologian as Harnack is compelled, by his fidelity to history, to admit: "Upon this surety alone, that the divine which appeared in Christ has the nature of the Godhead itself, can faith receive its power, life its law, and theology its direction." *

* "History of Dogma," Part II., Book I.

And, however loudly present-day critics may prophesy, Christianity knows its secret too well to attempt to confound its character with the secular demands of the age. There is no sign of an impending revolution. The hand that is laid upon the essential articles of Christianity is doomed to fall. Not a line has been erased from the Ecumenical Creeds of christendom. The Augustana of 1530—the venerable creed of the Reformation, of which Schaff says, "It struck the keynote of all the Evangelical Confessions," *—remains unchanged, and is to-day, perhaps, more authoritative than ever over its seventy-five million [half of the Protestant world] adherents. Nor is there the slightest movement to eliminate the christian essentials of doctrine from any of the more modern Christian creeds.

Modern Christianity, then, confronts the problems of the times and faces the future in a form identical with Primitive and Historic Christianity. Some may, indeed, sigh for the birth of a new Christianity, which knows no definite faith, but changes with every transient hue of thought, but we prefer to rest our confidence on the Rock that

* " Creeds of Christendom."

stands moveless amid the rise and ebb of seas. Nor do we believe that a Christianity shifting with every mood of thought is that in which men will trust. But a religion which is to bring them strength, comfort and peace can alone be one which will speak with no uncertain voice.

CONTRAST OF MODERNISM AND HISTORICAL CHRISTIANITY.

Between this historical conception of Christianity and that of the proposed new cast of theology there can be no agreement. The two views are irreconcilable. One offers us a natural, the other a supernatural Christianity. One proposes a human, the other a divine religion. One receives holy mysteries in faith, the other disowns them in the spirit of rationalism. One has a revealed and unique, the other an evolved and comparative Christianity. One has the Word of God, the other a mere ethical treatise. One has a Church with sacraments and means of grace, the other a mutually helpful society with symbolic ordinances. One speaks with the authority of Truth, the other claims unlimited liberty, since one opinion is no surer than another.

The one is historic, tracing its roots back to the

New Testament Age, the other boasts a "Modernism," from underneath which are cut the foundations of antiquity and history. The one has certainties and a surety of eternal life, the other "faintly trusts the larger hope." The one "puts away sin" by a propitiatory sacrifice, the other holds the Atonement unethical, and knows no remedy for sin. One meets and conquers death by a risen Saviour, the other sees the glorious Easter victory but an illusive myth. One opens the kingdom of heaven and secrets of the invisible world to believers, the other sees not behind the rayless wall.

One is positive, the other negative. One is conservative, the other revolutionary. One is constructive, the other destructive. Hence, there can be no compromise between these opposing views. They are mutually exclusive. They cannot coexist, for they would cease to subsist.

CONCLUSION.

Aye! Let us not yield our precious Christian birthright to the advance of this cold, destructive wave of skeptical criticism, lest we be driven to Matthew Arnold's despairing moan in that pathetic poem, where, "wild with all regret" he laments that—

> "The Sea of Faith
> Was once, too, at the full, and round earth's shore
> Lay like the folds of a bright girdle furl'd,
> But now I only hear
> Its melancholy, long, withdrawing roar,
> Retreating to the breath
> Of the mighty wind, down the vast edges drear,
> And naked shingles of the world.
>
> Ah, love, let us be true
> To one another! for the world which seems
> To lie before us like a land of dreams,
> So various, so beautiful, so new,
> Hath really neither joy, nor love, nor light,
> Nor certitude, nor peace, nor help for pain,
> And we are here as on a darkling plain,
> Swept with confused alarms of struggle and flight
> Where ignorant armies clash by night."

We do not, indeed, contend for an unchanging and identical historical Christianity—the *semper idem*—in the Romish sense, that the Church's expression of the faith cannot vary, or that new light on God's works may not aid to larger and deeper interpretations of His Word, or that Truth is not vital and endued with inherent power of growth and development, but we do hold that the great spiritual verities and eternal truths revealed by the Son of God are in their *essence* fixed and unalterable.

And that the Church must not waver in her confession of them to the end of time.

Christ Himself said of His revelation: "Heaven and earth shall pass away, but my words shall not pass away." *

And so, Primitive, Mediæval and Modern Christianity, and the Church of all ages and times, join in the sublime confession: The article of Faith, the ground of Hope, the object of Worship—"JESUS CHRIST, THE SAME YESTERDAY, AND TO-DAY, AND FOREVER." †

* Matt. xxiv. 35. † Heb. xii. 8.

www.ingramcontent.com/pod-product-compliance
Lightning Source LLC
Chambersburg PA
CBHW050334230426
43663CB00010B/1852